CHRISTOPHER GOODWINS

THE RAMBLINGS OF A COUNTRY CLERGYMAN

Bill Hedley Publications 2014

First published in July 2014
All rights reserved

Published in the U.K. by Bill Hedley Publications,
102 The Causeway, Isleham, Ely,
Cambridgeshire. CB7 5ST
Telephone: 01638 780284
Email: cwhgoodwins@gmail.com
Distribution by LULU, U.K.

ISBN 978-1-291-91658-4

Front cover: Cat
Designed by Bill Hedley.

Other publications by Christopher Goodwins

all available on Amazon

The New Testament In Limerick Verse
2001

**The Old Testament and The Apocrypha
In Limerick Verse**
2002

The Bible in Limerick Verse
*The whole bible in 1001 limericks,
including The Limerick Bible Hymn*
2006

The Motion Before You
Ten humorous skits on Church Council Meetings
2011

Lettus Tuh Tha Boy Jarn
100 humorous letters in Broad Norfolk
2013

I Was The Vicar
A sort of autobiography
2013

My Christian Faith
A comprehensive manual of Christian instruction
2013

CONTENTS

WHAT DO YOU THINK THIS BOOK
IS ALL ABOUT?

In 1956, when I drew the cat - the one that's featured on the front cover of this book - it was at a time in my life when I was most uncertain about the future.

I had completed the first of three years as a Choral Scholar at St. John's College Cambridge, and the ever-present prospects of failure in my BA Degree exams haunted me terribly. Furthermore, if I did eventually manage to graduate, all that *then* lay ahead of me was the uncertainty of two long years of National Service, and that really did increase the feeling of apprehension.

And at that stage, I had no idea at all about how my career would develop. In retrospect, a clue was stated at my first broadcast in 1950, when I said on Wilfred Pickles' BBC radio programme *'Have A Go!'* that, *"I would like to become a clergyman."* Little did I know how that prophesy would turn out to be true!

But back to the front cover. The cat is composed of a myriad of angular geometric brightly coloured shapes that seem to fit together - which are nothing like what a cat is meant to look like - but from an artistic point of view they seem to work.

This book, then, reflects the cat on the front cover. The chapters contain all sorts of unconnected thoughts and ideas that have buzzed around in my mind over the course of seventy-eight long years - since my distant beginnings in the wilds of Northumberland, in a little hamlet called Sparty Lea, to the Cambridgeshire village of Isleham where I now live, and where I shall most probably end my life on earth.

Included here, then, is poetry and drama, humour and satire, carols and hymns, liturgical experiments and history, things personal and things general - and hopefully, there should be at least *something* in this book that should interest you!

If it makes you think, then it will have achieved its purpose.

If it makes you smile, then I'm glad.

If it opens your eyes to a completely different way of looking at life, then the ramblings of a country clergyman will certainly not have been in vain!

So, are you ready to start?
Let's go!

Christopher Goodwins
Isleham, July 2014.

WILFRED PICKLES BRINGS *"HAVE A GO!"*
TO POTTER HEIGHAM

During lunch *(26 April 2003)* at The Crown Hotel, Watton, my school-friend of 50 years handed me a copy of the December edition of *"Let's Talk!"* On page 67 *(co-incidentally also my 67th birthday)* was a photograph of me, the dearest little smiling schoolboy, in a bright blue blazer, talking to Wilfred Pickles.

I had travelled by bus from Norwich to Potter Heigham that day because, as the 14-year old son of the Vicar, I had been selected to be one of the five contestants on the radio show, *"Have A Go!"* I remember that day as if it were yesterday, and all sorts of things happened which I would like to share with you, as the general public never knew about them until now.

At that time I was a School House boarder at Norwich School, and had been allowed to return home for the show - my very first broadcast. In those austere days after the war, there were certain luxuries at Boarding School that we tried to keep hidden from the weekly inspection of the prefects, such as the secret tin of Nestlé's Milk, hidden in the pocket of my mac that hung on the back of the study door.

I had completely forgotten about this, until, on the Number 5 bus to Potter Heigham, I reached for my ticket, only to discover to my horror that the whole of my mac pocket was drenched with sticky Nestlés Milk. There was nothing I could do about the situation except to *'stick it out'* until I got home, when my mother did a rapid laundry job on it, in time for me to wear it to the show, at Herbert Woods' Boat Yard canteen that evening.

Before the show, the producer, Barney Colehan, found out from me that I was Head Chorister and Treble Soloist in the Norwich School Choir, and suggested that I might like to sing something.

8

The only thing I could think of was the anthem, *"God be in my head,"* and I had just two minutes to find a scrap of newspaper, and write down the key words on it, such as *"Head, Eyes, Mouth, Heart, and End."*

I sang it unaccompanied, which normally wouldn't have presented a problem - except that the pianist, Violet Carson herself *(later to become the immensely famous Ena Sharples of Coronation Street)* had a go at an accompaniment. Being the little musical purist that I was at that time, I happened to pitch the note *between the semitones*. She tried accompanying me in one key, and that didn't work. So she tried another, and that didn't work either, and as she could see that I wasn't going to give in, she gave up!

So abandoning all further attempts, she let me continue unaccompanied. Wilfred Pickles then asked for a round of applause for me, saying that it was *"the nicest singing he'd ever heard on 'Have a Go!'"*

Normally, this would have gone un-noticed by most people. However, it happened that a man in London had his wireless on at the time of the broadcast, and had also come to the conclusion that it was the most beautiful singing that *he too* had ever heard, and sent me a couple of pounds as a reward for my efforts. That link developed into a ten-year friendship, and I spent a lot of time with him and his family in his London home.

He was none other than Lord Kennet, who had married Kathleen, the widow of the famous Captain Robert Falcon Scott of The Antarctic. I recall that he had the most distinguished handwriting, all the more astonishing, as he was left-handed. His right arm had been shot off at the battle of Zeebrugge when he was a young naval lieutenant.

Despite being severely wounded, he had continued casually manning the guns as if nothing had happened, with a cigar in his mouth, just like Churchill. He was decorated for bravery, and later on, in the world of politics, became Minister of Health.

In 1956 he bet me that I couldn't hitchhike to Northern Italy in less than ten days for less than ten pounds, to the villa where he was staying on holiday. So I teamed up with another Cambridge Geography student, a Girton College girl, and we did the journey in four days, for four pounds! It even included a night in a Paris hotel, where we had, just for the record, of course, *separate rooms!*

She left me at Nice, where I think *(subsequently proved to have been a wrong assumption)* that she was writing a thesis on Banditry in Corsica; and I stayed the next fortnight with the houseparty at Gli Scafari, Lerici, at the villa owned by Percy Lubbock, the then critic, essayist and biographer.

After that, we spent a week touring Tuscany, and another week in Guidecca, Venice. My reward for wining the *'bet'* not only included all that, but also my return train fare back from Venice to London - the route of the famous Orient Express - which was quite good to have won, just for having sung *'God Be In My Head'* on *'Have A Go!'*

On that programme, after telling Wilfred Pickles a little about myself, and how I hoped one day to be Ordained, I had to answer five simple questions on the noises that animals make.

All went well until the last question, which utterly stumped me: *"What noise do turkeys make, Christopher - or may I call you Chris?"* My mind went blank, and I risked losing something like twenty-five shillings if I couldn't come up with an answer.

10

But he was kindness itself, putting me out of my misery by asking, *"Well then - what noise do owls make?"* and I giggled to much applause, *"Hoot!"* Finally, he rewarded me with the well-known catch phrase, *"Give him the money, Barney!"*

You can now imagine what memories came back to me over lunch at Watton that day, when I saw the photograph in *"Let's Talk!"* I had been so excited that night, fifty-six years ago, and I remember my mother giving me some chocolate, to help me try to get to sleep.

It was all that she had in the house, poor dear, and it wouldn't have mattered much, except that its *brand name* rather gave the game away, relating to a very definite bodily function, with which most readers will be very familiar, namely *EXLAX!*

As a result of that first radio broadcast, later on in life I was privileged for seventeen years to be a member of the team of Epilogians at Plymouth who presented the last show of the day, *'Faith For Life'* on Westward TV, and *'Postscript'* on Television South West, in the days when TV wasn't continuous, but closed down late at night.

The *'Let's Talk!'* photograph evoked so many memories for me at Watton that lunchtime! It's very satisfying, now, to describe how my career developed as a result!

CHRISTOPHER'S SEVENTIETH BIRTHDAY

**I wrote a limerick for each person present,
and read them out at my 70th birthday lunch,
26 April 2006, at The White Pheasant, Fordham**

1. Now that I'm seventy years,
To **Doreen,** I raise my glass. Cheers!
How could I want more
Than my own dear *Dor Dor?*
For forty-six years, I've been *hers!*

2. We chose **Rupert** as our dear son,
And had him before he was one.
He's done jolly well,
You can see he looks swell -
And he's given us forty years' fun!

3. His son **Richard** followed his dad -
Spends hours at the keyboard, by gad!
When he gets his Degree,
I'll be seventy-three -
But we're all pretty proud of the lad!

4. **Louise** has come into our life,
And one day will be Rupert's wife.
Her knowledge and charm
Yes - she's Scottish - yes Ma'am,
And travelled to Fordham, from Fife!

5. Young **Marggie** - a bolt from the blue,
Came into our home - yes it's true!
Became like a daughter,
Till Mike came and caught her,
But Scotland has won her heart, *noo!*

6. Once, **Thomas,** the tank engine's fan
No longer a child, now a man;
The years have since passed,
And he's grown up so fast
We can hardly think how he began.

7. A partner for Marggie, this **Mike**
Acquired from Bob a motor bike.
To Dundee with care
He'll be motoring there -
Thursday and Friday. Some hike!

8. For sixty years, **David** and I
Have been friends, and this is no lie -
We've kept in touch so
That we feel that we know
What friendship should be. Hi there, hi!

9. Now **Brenda** is David's true love,
An angel, she came from above!
She keeps him in line,
And he thinks it's just fine,
So long as she gives him a shove!

10. We've known **Val,** a Lowestoft girl,
Her hair, then, with more than a curl;
Our daughter's godmother
There can be no other -
With quick repartee - she's a *pearl!*

11. Then **Paul** soon appeared on the scene,
A Lowestoft lad he had been.
When Val married him,
I announced the *wrong hymn,*
But jolly good friends we have been!

12. A Homerton lass, **Carole** - there -
A teacher, once Mayor, I swear!
Her Christmas cards say
'I'll write later.' No way -
It's always the same, every year!

13. A John's Choral Scholar, no less,
Was **Howard,** an Alto, confess -
Became our Best Man,
Got Ordained. Caravan
Takes them round the country, I guess.

14. In Church was where **Bob** and I met.
I baptised his daughter, the pet!
Coach driver - the best -
The Marina's his nest -
A Yamaha expert - you bet!

15. **Georgina** has been a good mate.
We meet every week, to create
A really new look
At each biblical book -
And always get home rather late!

16. Dear **Joan** was our neighbour next door
At Lowestoft, who could want more?
Although I'm now old,
Thank you Joan - heart of gold -
So good that you got here - *encore!*

17. Now **Stanley** had never been flying,
So one day, we went up - no lying.
The weight of us both
Created such sloth,
The engine prepared us for dying!

18. In church **Janice** welcomes us there;
Churchwarden, no less, I declare.
She ran the MU,
And she knows that it's true -
Her smile says it all! Yes - that's you!

19. The carrots **Brian** knew lots about,
As factory manager, no doubt.
But now he's retired,
Life has all been rewired -
The carrots are now *in the pot!*

20. So thank you for sharing this day
And coming from so far away.
Now, please raise your glasses
As time quickly passes,
And celebrate with me! *Olé!*

A PERSIAN PROVERB

**I came across this clever little poem many years ago,
and have often quoted it,
as I think it is full of common sense.**

1. He who *knows not,*
and *knows not* that he *knows not,*
is a fool ...
shun him.

2. He who *knows not,*
and *knows* that he *knows not,*
is ignorant ...
teach him.

3. He who *knows,*
and *knows not* that he *knows,*
is asleep ...
wake him.

4. He who *knows,*
and *knows* that he *knows,*
is a wise man ...
follow him!

THERE IS A GREEN HILL FAR AWAY

When I had a closer look at a map of England, I noticed that there was a hill, half a mile away from our house in Sparty Lea, in the wilds of Northumberland where I was born, and it was called *Green Hill*. It just gave me an idea, to re-write the famous hymn.

1. There is a Green Hill far away
Quite close to Sparty Lea
Where I was born, and lived, they say,
Till I was nearly three.

2. I did not know, nor could I tell
What life was like, up there.
But I believe that all went well,
With lots of love and care.

3. I had a nasty time, quite pale,
With whooping-cough for days.
But I survived to tell the tale,
Despite the doctor's gaze.

4. There were no other Goodwins near
The wilderness up there;
The winter's snow was so severe,
We had to live by prayer.

5. Oh, dearly do I love that place,
And some still love it too.
But nothing there now can replace
Our home, our home, with you.

G-PAWS: A MONTH IN THE LIFE OF PTUPPENCE

For my 78th birthday, I was given an amazing little gadget called G-PAWS. Measuring about an inch long, it records where a cat goes by day or night.

Intrigued by this, we bought a collar with a little bell on it (for Ptuppence, the kitten that adopted us in November 2013) - presumably so that it would warn any birds that were around - and attached the G-PAWS gadget to it. It is unaffected by temperature or wet weather, and fits into a bright orange plastic case that would be much easier to locate if it were to drop off.

My only fear is that - if the gadget were to get lost, or stolen - at £45 it would be an expensive tragedy, but it hasn't happened yet! Just for the record, the collar that she wears is loose enough to allow two fingers under it, so it's not too tight for her, and she seems to experience no anxiety at all in wearing it. In fact, we think that she rather likes her *'jewellery'!*

Up till now, we had absolutely no idea where Ptuppence might go when she was out of the house, and assumed, wrongly, that she just stayed in the garden, or maybe strayed into the next-door neighbour's gardens. To our surprise, when we detached the gadget at the end of the day, and plugged it into my laptop computer, we were astonished to see *not only* how far she had travelled, but *where* she had actually gone!

G-PAWS has the option of producing her track superimposed upon a birds' eye view of the village, or on a conventional map, in both cases with all the streets named. On the first morning that we inspected her walkabouts, it was evident that she had not only left the safe haven of our front garden, but had actually crossed the busy main road no less than fifteen times!

There were three main areas of interest for Ptuppence, that varied from day to day. On the first day, it was our garden area, northwards across the road, and into the back gardens of the houses there; and then secondly, to the left of our bungalow westwards - about two hundred yards altogether.

On subsequent days, we were amazed to find that for her third area of exploration she had travelled a considerable way into the field south of our bungalow, and even more dramatic, northwards again over the main road and across the gardens of several houses opposite, and into the lane leading to the allotments - a distance of about half a mile!

G-PAWS records the distance Ptuppence travels in kilometres, and also the average speed. The latter proves to be most unreliable, as it recorded speeds between 3mph and 73mph! However, the distances seemed to be fairly accurate - from the signals transmitted from satellite GPS, and in the first three days, she notched up over eleven and a half miles!

If she continued at that rate, she would travel the unbelievable distance of 1400 miles a year! For the past month I have plotted the results each day on my laptop spreadsheet, and converted kilometres to miles, and kph to mph to make it easier to analyse.

For the past five years, I have accompanied a friend on his daily walks around the village - such exercise being a requirement for those of us with diabetes. Before I experimented with Ptuppence, I carried the G-PAWS gadget with me, in my shirt top pocket, and it recorded our walkabout with amazing accuracy. I suppose that I could have attached it to my clerical *dog-collar!*

We found that, when it was used for the first time, it initially took about 15 minutes to link up with the satellites, but after that, only about two or three minutes. So there are occasions when it doesn't start recording the first few hundred yards - but that doesn't alter the fact that it is an amazing instrument, and great fun to analyse afterwards!

It has all sorts of possibilities other than recording the cat's travels. For example, it could be standard issue for wives who were suspicious of their husbands' movements. When he says that he has been out for a walk, she will knew within minutes on his return whether he has been telling the truth or not, as the G-PAWS may have clearly indicated a journey only to the local pub and back instead!

So - I thoroughly recommend G-PAWS as a present for someone, as it produces hours of fun and interest, that would otherwise remain a complete mystery about where one's pets get to (or husbands - or, for that matter, wives or children) when they go out!

Miaow!

DOREEN'S SEVENTIETH BIRTHDAY

This was the poem I wrote for the occasion of Doreen's 70th birthday, and which was read out at the Dunkeld Hilton Hotel dining room, Scotland, in the presence of the invited guests.

1. For forty seven years we've been together
In rain and sun - indeed all sorts of weather;
And now you've reached your threescore years and ten,
The time has flown, we don't know where or when.

2. From Cambridge days at Homerton, you learned
To inspire East End girls, who Geog spurned.
'Do as I say, instead of what I do'
Has brought the natural teacher out in you.

3. In all that time, you've mellowed and become
A friend, a mother, wife, light of our home.
Although your aches and pains restrict your life,
Your wit is still as sharp as sharpest knife.

4. In politics, the Liberals took your vote,
At Harrogate, your maiden speech, of note!
You always seem to find the words to say,
And London humour often saves the day!

5. Of many things you're expert at, by far
Your cooking well deserves a Michelin star.
In fact, your fame exporting Christmas puddings
Has made your name worldwide, O Mrs Goodwins.

6. In recent years, from watercolour toil
Your art branched out with portraits done in oil.
And cross-stitch cards at Festivals by dozens
You send to family, friends, and distant cousins.

7. Your faith has been your mainstay from your youth,
And passionate concern to seek the truth.
Two books are in the pipeline, from your heart
Awaiting publication, works of art.

8. An expert driver, with the IAM
And Chairman of the Plymouth Group, ahem!
To every continent you've been, save one,
And nearly sixty countries we have done,

9. Made possible with your electric scooter,
With forward, and reverse with bleeping hooter.
So, Doreen, on this most auspicious day
Supported by your friends and family,

10. From north and south, from east and west we've come
To share your happy day, and drink your rum:
Congratulations - it's our love you've won!
So, raise your glass, and toast my Number One!

THE 2005 PHARADAY LECTURE
at St. John's College, Cambridge

I heard something like this at a concert when I was at Lincoln Theological College, delivered by a student with a broad Germanic accent, and thought this much-extended version funny enough to deserve to be included here!

A full list of references to the words in italics - found in hymns, psalms, and prayerbooks - is available on request.

I am of all men the most honoured to be invited to give the Saint John's College Choir Association first Pharaday Lecture in June, for this *august* magazine. My subject is naturally that of Jerusalem.

One tends to grow up thinking that Jerusalem is *a land flowing with milk and honey.* While this is no doubt true, have you ever considered from where comes *the honey?*

My first startling revelation is that it is *not the labours of my hands,* but that the honey indeed comes from *the bees.* "What bees?" I hear you ask. Well, you will not know that there are many, many varieties of bees in that part of the world.

Most common of all is *the glory be.* One will find *the glory be* usually at the end of *the psalm,* and always at the top of the date-tree. *The glory bees* are not to be confused with *the lovely be,* nor with *the evermore shall be.*

Nor, on a Sunday, with *the father be,* because it is clearly different in colour and type from *the pure and spotless let us be,* which preys on all the others.

There is also *the endless prayer be,* associated with *the outward vesture be.* In passing, I shall mention only briefly *the constant be, the servant be, the words and actions be, the blessing be,* and I forget the name of the other one. . . ah yes - I remember it now - the *lest I forgetful be!* And there is also *the eternally be.*

Big fleas have little fleas upon their backs to bite them. And little fleas have lesser fleas, and so ad infinitum. Here I would mention only *the vain shadows flee,* and one other - *the comforts flee,* with which one would associate such creatures in that part of the world, and which I will show later to be of great help to the *Judah's lion.* Have you come across *the sinful flee?* And there is also *the bidding fly,* and the very strange *bosom fly,* the soul of which tends to *cleave to the dust.*

But, my friends, back to *the bees.* And what is it that steals the honey from the bees? It is, of course, *the bears.* If they didn't steal so much, *earth shall then her fruits afford!* You remember the old telly advert, where 'all the bears love the honey, mummy.' Sadly, not all bears have such good natures.

There is, for example, *gladly the cross-eyed bear.* He sees not the honey that he eats, because he cannot see straight ahead. There are *bears and forbears,* of course, such as *the staff to bear.* Best known of all the bears is the little favourite of the Mayor's dear wife, Grace. Ah, dear Sheba! *Can a woman's tender care cease towards the child she bare?*

And, if you enjoy the clubbing downtown, you must certainly see *the dazzling body bears, the gently bears,* and *the angels bear.* And *the rolling stream bears* are also a sight to behold, but you must beware in case *the wolves devour thy fold!* And if they do catch you, you will much *sorrow bear!* Watch out, also, for *the cross he-boar!* and the *cross exalted boar, too.* And *let every creature rise and bring peculiar honours.*

But what about *the sloth?* One needs to be kept *safe from sloth. The dull sloth* is really dull, my friends, simply because of his tummy pains, from eating *the sudden greens and herbage crowned. Judah's lion,* however, suffers not the tummy bug, but is greatly helped by *the comforts flee,* of which I have spoken much already. *Judah's lion* was so strong that when *he burst his chains,* he *fell on a serpent, and crushed its head!*

Leaving aside the animals for a moment, you may know that Jerusalem is much given to the manufacture of automobiles these days. The Mayor's brother, Victor, once went in for a raffle. And *when the strife was o'er, and the battle done, now is the Victor's Triumph won,* he gave it to Ernest as a present, but soon abandoned it for a new Honda. "Now then, s*hall we madly cast away?"* suggests the Mayor.

We have the big Honda factory here in Jerusalem, as you will recall. *There, in one grand Acclaim* is the limousine in which you see the Mayor of Jerusalem riding around, after he got a bit fed up with the *high Triumph.* He just about tolerated its suspension, *smooth let it be or rough.*

He happens also to like flying, and was a great *lover of Concord,* and also of *the winged squadrons of the sky,* but for *those whose course on earth is over,* he has been known to switch his car allegiance to *Sunbeams scorching all the day.*

He had to give that one up too, when it developed *manifold temptations*. *"Thy friendly crook,"* he said to the garage owner, *"shall give me aid!"*

The Mayor's wife, you may already know, is the beautiful Grace. Oh, *give us Grace!* He much prefers her to his old flame, *mystic Rose*. That's *the Rose that cannot wither*. But ah, Grace! What a woman she is! Grace is just fantastic - *amazing Grace,* and she *never fails from age to age!*

She has an ambitious young nephew, *Ernest,* who is *always looking forward,* despite his *night of doubt and sorrow.* Ernest had *hoped to follow Julie,* but another of his girlfriends, *Dawn, in the slow watches of the night, had already ensured that the flags had appeared on the hills, long cold and grey,* at least, *on the purple-headed mountain.*

So *Dawn leads on another day, wakened by the solemn warning.* He cups his hands, and calls out to her, *"Keep love's banner floating o'er you!"* - but she didn't hear what he had said. *"Fling out the banner!* he yells to her once again.

And so you see that Jerusalem has many great attractions for those who love the creatures great and small, and where *all the creatures own their sway. It is a land of pure delight!*

My friends, I trust that you have enjoyed my lecture this year about the wonderful city of Jerusalem? I look forward to addressing you all again next year!

Good night!

Professor Sniwdoog Hw Rehpotsirch
(St. John's College, Cambridge, 1955-1958)

26

THE BROADLAND HYMN

(to the tune 'Almsgiving' - Number 480
in the Ancient & Modern Revised Hymnal.).

Written by my father,
The Reverend Bernard Myddleton Goodwins,
MA(Dunelm), 1894-1980,
when he was Vicar of Potter Heigham,
and Repps-cum-Bastwyck, Norfolk.

1. O Lord of woodland, marsh, and field,
To Thee our praise and thanks we yield
For art and Majesty revealed,
  Who madest all.

2. To skies above our homesteads fair.
We lift our eyes, and read Thee there,
Yet feel Thy presence everywhere,
  Who seest all.

3. Our fathers delved with might and main
These fruitful lands to dyke and drain,
As Thou didst bless their soil with gain,
  So bless us Lord.

4. For beast and bird which give us food,
For Home and Mart, and all men's good,
We say our Grace, as children should,
  And thank Thee, Lord.

5. These pleasant ways are not for greed
Of rod, or gun, or wanton speed.
May we, when from our duties freed,
  Use them aright.

6. Bless, Lord, our homes, our work, our friends,
Prosper the Church that each attends,
Fit us for Life which never ends,
       With Thee above.

7. Though in green pastures here we dwell,
The choice is ours, of Heaven, or Hell:
O give us Grace to choose right well,
       The Heavenly Way.

8. So bid us, Lord, be of good cheer,
Each day and night, and year by year,
Thy rod and staff will comfort fear,
       When journey's done.

9. O Lord of woodland, marsh, and field,
To Thee our praise and thanks we yield.
But most for Love in Christ revealed,
       Who lovest all.

GRUMPY OLD MAN'S FIRST ARTICLE

**My first *Grumpy Old Man's article,* was written for the
St. John's College Cambridge Choir Association
1999 Magazine**

When excellent Choirs sing excellent music excellently,
it's always *such a let-down* when the whole thing is then
spoiled by the *awful* singing of the *Clergy!*

I have listened to so many broadcasts over the years, where
anybody with even an ounce of presentational intelligence
should be able to see that, if the Precentor's part, the
Clergyman's part, the Cantor's part, cannot be sung *as
beautifully as the rest of the singing,* then he should be big
enough to admit it, and hand the job over to someone else
who *can* sing beautifully.

Having been a supporter for the last fifty-three years of all
that the Royal School of Church Music has been trying to
achieve in this respect, I feel deeply saddened that its
influence has hardly touched parish churches or the great
Cathedrals and Colleges. Places with superb musical
traditions are *still* so often lumbered with *the bad singing of
the Clergy.*

For example, *the Responses.* Clergy who attempt to intone
these should be encouraged to do so *at least at speech
rhythm.* There is absolutely no need to become quaintly
parsonical about the Responses. They are really quite easy
to sing, and don't need Clergy to make a mess of them.
Why not ask a competent layman? And if the Old Chap,
who has been doing the Cantor's job for years and years,
simply can't see that it is *his* singing which is spoiling the
excellence of the rest of the occasion, then someone really
ought to find a way of telling him politely that *it's time he
gave up!*

However, what makes it *really difficult* to bring about such change is that, while some of these Clergy are in very senior positions in their own establishments, they are often also great supporters of their Choirs and Choral traditions, and because of that, no one dare upset the Old Chap, in case he then withdraws his support.

Where we are striving for excellence in the Choral tradition, the Clergy who are privileged to take part really ought, like anybody else, to undergo a proper voice trial at least once a year, have the graciousness to step down if they don't pass the test, and *then* let someone else who *can* sing beautifully take their place. There are many Clergy about with excellent singing voices, who would be only too happy to be invited to take on such a role. All too often, however, just because the Precentor, Cantor, or whatever has been in office there for years and years, no one dare upset him! This *can't* be right!

Now, - surely this is an area which concerns all the great Choral traditions of our Cathedrals and Colleges? Surely any Clergyman with even an ounce of common sense and decency should be among the first to have the courage to approach their Musical Directors, or to seek independent advice from some other Musical Director, to determine whether or not his singing is up to the standard of the Choir of that place?

If you want to test the validity of this argument, just listen to the next lot of broadcasts of Choral Evensong, or go along to any of the great Cathedrals and Colleges and hear for yourself how Clergy so frequently *let the side down.*

It is a great eye opener, I assure you. Having been most concerned about this matter since I first became a member of the Royal School of Church Music in 1946, - and incidentally, having noticed it *all the more* after Ordination as a Clergyman of the Church of England 35 years ago, and from the vantage point of having been a Choral Scholar of St. John's as well, - I feel I do have a right to express my opinions on the matter.

One final note - for any Clergy reading this article. If you are not sure whether I'm getting at *you,* in what I have said above, then please pluck-up the courage to go and ask someone to test you out at once. And if your singing really *is* dreadful - and there *are* plenty of you out there who *do sing dreadfully* - then please have the graciousness to *step down,* and hand over the singing to someone else, who *can* sing beautifully. Or just *say* it instead!

We talk about giving God *the best* in worship: well, here's a chance for us to prove it, - and to improve the quality of our great Choral tradition of worship sung beautifully! Whatever you do, though, - please don't take umbrage if you are told gently that your singing is *not good enough.* What we sing has got to be *the best* for God, and *not the second best!*

**Christopher Goodwins
1999**

THE ISLEHAM FENLAND HYMN

In 2004, I decided to match my father's *Broadland Hymn* with my own *Isleham Fenland Hymn*. So far as I know, it's the only hymn ever written that mentions *carrots, sugar beet and onions!*

(To be sung to the 1st tune of AMR 26 - 'God that madest earth and heaven,' or, if more adventurous, and much preferred - to the tune of A&M New Standard 457, 'East Acklam,' - 'For the fruits of his creation.')

1.   God, who made the whole creation
      We worship You.
      God, whose love for every nation
      Made us like You.
      For the Fenland - once the sea shore,
      Drained, reclaimed, and made into
      A fertile garden - Modern Eden,
      We worship You.

2.   Once we ploughed by means of horses,
      Now by machine.
      Where the land was drained by windmills,
      Pumps now are seen.
      Combines do the work so fast,
      And time goes by and doesn't rest,
      But we give thanks to God our Father -
      We worship You.

3.   Carrots, sugar beet, and onions
      Grow all around.
      Shops, and school, and industry
      And houses abound.
      Work together, loving neighbour,
      Putting God first brings us closer
      To the way our Saviour wants us
      To worship Him.

4.   At our Church, *Saint Andrew's, Isleham,
         We worship You.
         With our Christian friends around us
         We follow You.
         Holy Spirit guide us always,
         Be our strength and comfort as we
         Give our best to our Lord Jesus -
         Come, Lord, today!

Written by me when I was Priest-In-Charge of Isleham, Cambridgeshire, 1999 to 2004, and dedicated to St. Andrew's Church on the occasion of my final service there.

* The name of your own parish church may be substituted.

BISHOP JOHN WILLIAM COLENSO
(28 January 1814 - 20 June 1883)

For many years, I have been fascinated by the way in which Bishop Colenso was *(wrongly)* vilified by both Church and State, when all he was trying to do was to seek the truth about what the Bible said. This essay commemorates the 200th anniversary of his birth.

Only about a hundred and sixty* years ago, *(about 1854)* a student of mathematics at St John's College Cambridge – *an exhibitioner, then scholar, who was placed Second Wrangler in his final exams, and in 1837 immediately elected a Fellow -.* was consecrated Bishop in Westminster Abbey on 30th November *1853.

He became the first Bishop of Natal, with the object of converting the natives to Christianity. His first job was to translate the Bible into Zulu. So, with the help of his native boys, he began - *where anyone else would have begun in those days* - with Genesis, and methodically worked his way along the first few books of the Old Testament.

The more he translated, the more concerned he became, about the way in which the narrative seemed to be *"honeycombed with impossibilities."* But he persevered, because he had to get the job done.

However, because he had been a mathematician at Cambridge University, he was naturally interested wherever the bible mentioned *numbers or measurements.*

At first, just for his own interest, *(mostly between 1861 and 1879)* he began calculating the dimensions of the Ark (Genesis 6:15), and got the shock of his life! He said, "How could Noah's flat bottomed Ark have survived at all, tossed about in water several miles deep *(if it covered the face of the earth, it was at least five miles deep, covering Everest!)*

And yet, after a year, there's a dove around who can manage to find an olive branch *still green and alive,* which must have survived, at *that* depth of water, *after a year's flood!"*

A Bishop of the *Church of England by law Established* was duty bound to concern himself with *the truth,* and Colenso had to say to himself, "Is all that *really true?* Do you really *believe* that *all the animals* came in to the Ark, and that they came in *in pairs?* And that Noah was able to gather food for them *all* - food for the beasts and birds of prey, as well as for the rest!"

He had a brother in Australia, to whom he wrote, asking about his sheep farm. How much acreage would two average sheep need for a year's grass? Colenso was puzzled about this. How did Noah manage to collect just that item alone, *the grass* - never mind the rest of the things?

And what about the wingless birds of New Zealand or Australia? How did *they* come into the Ark? The incredible answer to that, he suggested, must have been that they never came into the Ark at all, but that God created them afresh when the waters had subsided! But the Bible doesn't say that!

Colenso's native boy had an elephant – quite a hefty beast. The weight of this one elephant alone would nearly have sunk the Ark *(with that given displacement of water)* - let alone *a pair of elephants!*

And the biblical narrative doesn't suggest how Noah managed to collect the *rest* of the animals, birds, creeping things, human beings, food, and so on – and he was therefore forced to conclude that the whole thing seemed to be quite incredible!

In Genesis 38, he worked out that Hezron and Hamul must have been great-grandsons of a man aged only 42; which, assuming that each man had produced a male child at 10-and-a-half years old, and even allowing for primitive fertility, was still a feat quite beyond normal imagination!

Then he went on to tackle the whole story of The Exodus. The marvels of the feats performed by Moses and Aaron, and also by the Egyptian magicians of Pharaoh, just had to be seen to be believed! Serpents, water turning to blood, plagues of frogs, lice, flies, cattle diseases, and boils, hail and fire, locusts, all capped by three days of darkness: this was pretty clever to have been achieved!

But it was nothing compared with the administrative problems involved in the Exodus itself. The dividing of the Sea was *some feat,* decided Colenso. So also was the quality of Moses' command, for he estimated that there must have been around *two-and-a-half million people* involved!

The number of men - aged over 20 years, able to bear arms – is quoted in the bible as being 603,550. Allowing a wife each *(they married earlier than we do),* and two children each - plus the elderly, plus the bachelors and spinsters outside those categories, must have amounted to *about two-and-a-half million* - plus flocks and herds, and *'very much cattle'* - all this must have taken some shifting!

Even so, at midnight, *they rose to a man,* and moved off towards the Red Sea, where they camped ready for the crossing.

Each man had to carry a lot of baggage. Assuming that they dwelt in *booths,* from where did they get the boughs and bushes needed for the purpose? From the wilderness where they were camped?

So assuming, instead, that they carried *tents,* at the very least they would have needed 200,000 tents for a population of over two-and-a-half million! Had these tents been provided in expectation of marching? Especially when you realise that the request that Moses had put to Pharaoh had been only to be allowed to go away for *a three days' journey!*

Anyway, how could they *carry* the tents, even assuming that they had them? Their backs were loaded with dough and kneading-troughs already as it was, together with enough grain for one month - there being no manna until the 16th day of the second month! Perhaps the oxen carried it.

But an ox could carry only four light tents, and certainly no more than one skin tent. Therefore, by that reckoning, two hundred thousand oxen would have been required. But here's another snag: oxen need training, and will not carry loads on their backs, if not *trained* to do so!

The camp itself must have been vast! To house all those people, and cattle, and herds, and flocks - allowing four square yards only for each person - the camp must have covered more than 1650acres, which is about the size of a city 12 miles square – in other words, as big as Greater London!

Furthermore, according to Levitical direction, the priest was duty bound to carry away all the daily refuse - all the sacrificial entrails, dung, and so on - outside the perimeter at the camp, and burn it there before nightfall. The logistics of this feature alone, and the strength of the priest concerned, must have been miraculous!
It would have required him to do a six-mile run with a loaded wheelbarrow, and then back again! One priest on his own would never have done it!

And what about the midwives? For a camp numbering nearly three million people, only *two* midwives are mentioned. This is emphasised, by virtue of the fact that we are especially given their names – Shiprah and Puah!

Moses and Aaron are said to have addressed *the whole assembly of the people.* But what human voice *(even nowadays)* could make itself heard at any one time by *about two-and-a-half million people?*

They are said to have all congregated *'in front of the door of the tent of meeting.'* Remembering that the court measured only 18 by 34 ft, it would have held a maximum capacity of five hundred people. However, some 600,550 warriors are said to have stood there! Assuming that they stood shoulder to shoulder, in a row 9 across, that column of men alone would have stretched for *more than 21 miles!* So 'what are we to understand by all this?' thought Colenso.

Moving on to other books in the Bible, Colenso came across the story of Balaam's ass. Can anyone believe that the ass had *the gift of articulate speech?* Never before or since has this incidence been known!

And what about the way that Joshua caused the sun, and also the moon, *to stand still for a whole day!* From what we know now of gravity, if he *really had managed to achieve that astronomical feat,* gravity would no longer have been able to hold us down – and we would all have been sucked-off into space.

Referring back to Genesis, Joseph is said to have sent to his father ten she-asses laden with the good things of Egypt - corn, bread, and victuals. But even if these asses were fully laden, they could not be expected to carry enough food for a thousand servants, besides Jacob's own children - *for a period of 12 months,* which was *also* a time of famine!

38

And again, in the narrative about The Exodus, there were 603,550 *men* mentioned, all of whom were *armed!* In which case, is it not a surprising thing that all these warriors allowed themselves to be kept down in Egypt, without considering any military resistance?

Is it any wonder that in 1867, 11,500 English clergy signed a petition to have Colenso excommunicated? Even the Prime Minister, and Parliament, and the Privy Council became involved in what they considered to be – for The Church, as well as for The Establishment - *an enormously dangerous scandal.* In the quest for truth, Bishop Colenso was *(wrongly)* assumed to be demolishing the very foundations upon which they rested. This was only 1866 - a mere 147* years ago!

Today, people are often heard to say, *"So you surely don't believe all that you read in the bible?"*

It's very important to stress that this wasn't Colenso's stance at all: as a Church of England Bishop, all he was guilty of was *for being absolutely passionate to discover the truth,* and to determine whether there might well be *another meaning, other than a literal meaning,* to what he found in the text of the bible.

Knowing this background about Colenso – on whose side would *you* have been, about 160 years ago? *Or on* whose side would *you* be, *even today!*

*Most of the above was gleaned from
the 2-volume biography
of Bishop John Colenso,
by Sir G. W. Cox (1988), London.*

39

THE HARVEST HYMN

*(Composed by The Reverend Peter Wright,
lecturer at Lincoln Theological College, 1964)*

1. We plough the fields with tractors,
With drills we sow the land.
But growth is still the wondrous gift
Of God's almighty hand.
He sends the snow in winter,
The warmth to swell the grain,
The breezes and the sunshine,
And soft refreshing rain.
> *All good gifts around us
> Are sent from Heaven above:
> So thank the Lord,
> O thank the Lord,
> For all His love.*

2. With many new machines now
We do the work each day.
We reap the fields with combines,
We bale the new mown hay.
But it is God who gives us
Inventive skills and drives,
Which lighten labour's drudgery,
To give us better lives.
> *All good gifts &c.*

3. We thank You then, O Father,
For all things bright and good:
The seed time and the harvest,
Our life, our health, our food.
Accept the gifts we offer,
For all Your love imparts,
But what You most desire is
The love of thankful hearts.
> *All good gifts &c.*

TEN NEW CHRISTMAS CAROLS

The idea came to me many years ago, that we ought to have carols at Christmas that really were *based much more upon the Bible.* With that in mind, I wrote these ten new carols, composed the music, and recorded myself singing them on a CD *(available from me, on request).*

Some of them are amusing, and lovely to sing, and would certainly appeal to children, as well as to adults.

As with other traditional Christmas carols, *I too* have used *'poetic licence'* on occasions – as they do - but my aim was to try to stick to the text as far as possible.

No one to my knowledge, however, has ever attempted to put *The Christmas Gospel* into poetry, or even to set it to music. Whereas my own version *(Carol 5)* is by no means perfect, it does at least put John chapter 1, verses 1 to 14 into musical form, possibly for use at a Carol Service.

It is my hope that *Carol 1* will be useful for anybody trying to remember *who said what* about The Nativity, in the Gospel records.

Two carols are set to very popular secular tunes: *Carol 2* to *'Jingle Bells,'* and Carol 4 to *'I'm dreaming of a white Christmas.'* People should enjoy singing those, and might even be persuaded to think seriously about the meaning of the words, which are more committing – in a Christian sense - than those of many traditional carols.

So – I hope that you enjoy these new carols, and look forward to receiving your comments.

11 September 2008

1. MATTHEW TELLS ABOUT THE WISE MEN

1. Matth-ew tells about the Wise Men,
   Matth-ew tells about the star.
      Tells about the star that led the
      Wise Men to Bethlehem,
   Shining still for you and me.

2. Matth-ew tells how crafty Herod
   Tried to trick the three Wise Men.
      Asked them to discover where the
      Baby was in Bethlehem:
   They would worship, so could he.

3. Matth-ew tells about the gifts of
   Gold and frankincense and myrrh,
      Tells about the presents brought to
      Jesus by the Wise men,
   How they took the safe way home.

4. Lu-ke tells about the manger,
   Lu-ke tells about the inn,
      Tells about the angels singing
      Halle-halleluia,
   Bethlehem had no more room.

5. Lu-ke tells about the census,
   Lu-ke tells how Mary gave
      Birth to baby Jesus there and
      Wrapped him in a blanket,
   Kept him warm for all to see.

6. Matth-ew tells how wicked Herod
   Killed all the babes in Bethlehem
           Two years old and under, except
           Little baby Jesus, who
   Escaped to Egypt, His new home.

7. Matth-ew wrote for Jewish people,
   Lu-ke wrote for you and me,
           All we need to know of
           Baby Jesus born at Bethlehem:
   Saviour of the world is He!

           All we need to know of
           Baby Jesus born at Bethlehem:
           Saviour of the world is He!

2. JINGLE BELLS

1. When Joseph travelled down
   From Nazareth his town,
   He was far too late to find a place
   Where Mary and he could stay.
   The inn was full that night,
   And the landlord had a fright -
   One look at Mary made it clear
   That a baby was on its way! Oh -
   > *Christmas Eve, Christmas Day,*
   > *Jesus comes again!*
   > *Every day, and in every way*
   > *Jesus comes to reign! Oh -*
   > *Christmas Eve, Christmas Day,*
   > *Jesus comes to stay!*
   > *In our hearts*
   > *We're glad to welcome*
   > *Jesus Christ today!*

2. So the landlord scratched his head,
   "If you think I've got a bed,"
   He said, *"There's a stable round the back,*
   You can look at that instead."
   So Joseph had a word
   With Mary. *"How absurd!"*
   She said, *"No choice!"* then she lost her voice -
   To the stable they were led. Oh -
   > *Christmas Eve, Christmas Day, &c.*

3. It was later on that night,
   When the stars were shining bright,
   Mary produced a baby boy
   In the stable, on the hay.
   She cuddled him and thought
   That if only she had brought
   Some baby clothes, and this and that -
   What a memory she had got! Oh -
   Christmas Eve, Christmas Day, &c.

4. The travellers asked around,
   And lots of things they found
   For the little boy
   Who was born on the hay
   With the animals all around.
   Poor Joseph's face went red -
   He'd forgotten to look ahead,
   And here was a boy, not a single toy!
   But he was a proud proud dad! Oh -
   Christmas Eve, Christmas Day, &c

5. So back they travelled home,
   Singing *'Nazareth, here we come!'*
   And Joseph was a very proud dad,
   And Mary was a happy mum!
   When they came to give Him a name,
   Only one Word to them came -
   It was 'Jesus,' born in Bethlehem
   In a manger full of hay! Oh -

   > *Christmas Eve, Christmas Day,*
   > *Jesus comes again!*
   > *Every day, and in every way*
   > *Jesus comes to reign! Oh -*
   > *Christmas Eve, Christmas Day,*
   > *Jesus comes to stay!*
   > *In our hearts*
   > *We're glad to welcome*
   > *Jesus Christ today!*

   > *In our hearts*
   > *We're glad to welcome*
   > *Jesus Christ today!*

3. CAESAR AUGUSTUS

1. Caesar Augustus
   Made a decree:
   All the world
   Shall pay me
   > Taxes, taxes, taxes, taxes,
   > Taxes, tacketty, tax.

2. Joseph came
   From Nazareth
   In Galilee
   Where his family
   > Lived at Bethlehem, lived at Bethlehem,
   > Lived at Bethlehem.

3. Mary was
   Great with child,
   Travelled too,
   Luggage piled
   > On a donkey, donkey, donkey donkey
   > Donkey, donketty, donk.

4. Gave birth to
   Baby new:
   "Manger straw -
   Cot for You!"
   > Loved Him, loved Him, loved Him,
   > loved Him, Loved Him,
   > loved Him, Love.

5. Inn was full,
   Stable bed
   Was the Babe's
   Home instead
   > With the animals, animals, animals,
   > animals, animals, animals, an.

6.   Shepherds raced
           To the scene.
           Sheep content,
           Pastures green:
                    Joseph, Mary; Jesus, manger;
                    Angels, glory, and praise!

7.   We know well
           He was born
           That Nowell,
           Christmas morn:
                    Baby, Teacher, Saviour, Spirit
                    Love is born today!

                    Baby, Teacher, Saviour, Spirit
                    Love is born today!

4. WHITE CHRISTMAS

1. We're following the Lord Jesus,
   We're his disciples day by day;
   Whether life is easy, or hard,
   That's when Jesus Christ becomes our Lord.
   At Bethlehem, the inn-keeper
   Had nowhere but a stable shed.
   And that's where our Saviour was born -
   Just the manger hay to rest His head.

2. Wise men brought gold with frankincense,
   And myrrh - the strangest gift of all.
   Yet the Gospel needs it to be
   Something royal for Christ's nativity.
   This makes us all the more conscious
   That Christian life demands a lot,
   But when Jesus Christ is our Lord,
   Then we're glad to give Him all we've got!

3. The shepherds stared in sheer wonder,
   Joseph and Mary couldn't see
   That if God could come to mankind -
   Then His birth must be humility.
   We're challenged now to say if we
   Believe in Jesus Christ our Lord.
   Because we're either for, or against,
   And we can't pretend that we've not heard!

4. All Christians therefore join forces,
   We put Christ Jesus first in life!
   He transforms each heart with His touch,
   Millions testify His power is such!"
   We're following the Lord Jesus,
   We're His disciples day by day,
   Whether life is easy or hard,
   Jesus Christ will always be our Lord!

   Jesus Christ will always be our Lord!

5. IN THE BEGINNING WAS THE WORD

1. In the beginning was the Word:
   That's another name for Jesus!

2. The Word was with God, and the Word was God:
   That's another name for Jesus!

3. He was there at the start of the world:
   That's the God we see in Jesus!

4. All things around were made by Him:
   God the Creator, in Jesus!

5. In Him was Life, and the Light of men:
   That's the way to live - like Jesus!

6. He lit up the dark, as the Light of the world:
   Shine on us! Shine on, Jesus!

7. A man came from God, and his name was John:
   Wrote the Gospel facts about Jesus!

8. *He* was not the Light, but a witness to the Lord:
   He told us to believe in Jesus!

9. God was in the world, and the world was made by Him:
   That's the God we see in Jesus!

10. He came to His own, but they received Him not:
    That's what we did to Jesus!

11. But those who received Him became His friends:
    What a Friend we have in Jesus!

12. All of them became the children of God:
    In the fellowship of Jesus!

13. So the Word became flesh, and He lived on this earth:
    We beheld the glory of Jesus!

14. God became man through the power of His Spirit:
    That's why we believe in Jesus!
        That's why we believe in Jesus!

6. OFF WE GO TO BETHLEHEM

1. Off we go to Bethlehem,
       Just to see
       Baby Jesus.
Mary placed Him
       In a manger,
       Sleeping
       In peace.

2. What did we expect to see?
       Crowded inn,
       Lots of strangers.
No more room
       Even the
       Stable was
       all booked-up.

3. Joseph had to register:
       Bethlehem
       His ancestral seat.
His family
       Now was three
       Instead of
       Just two.

4. What were shepherds
       Doing there?
       Angels too
       Singing 'Halleluia
Peace, and goodwill
       To all people
       On earth.'

5. They proclaimed Him
        God as man,
        Born for us,
Lighting up the
        Darkness, so that we
        May follow Jesus,
        Our Lord!

7. O JO-SEPH! O JO-SEPH!

1. O Jo-seph! O Jo-seph!
We've got to go to Beth-le-hem.
Get the donkey out,
Pack the luggage up,
Wave goodbye to Naz-a-reth!

2. O Mar-y! O Mar-y!
It's a very bumpy road, I know -
But it won't take long
If we sing a song
As we travel to Beth-le-hem.

3. O Jo-seph! O Jo-seph!
I can see the lights of an inn ahead!
If there's no room there
I'll sleep on the floor -
Just find somewhere to rest my head!

4. O Mar-y! O Mar-y!
It's full up, my dear, so round that way
Is the oxen shed,
And the only bed
Is the stable, with some nice fresh hay!

5. O Jo-seph! O Jo-seph!
Anything at all will do, tonight!
I'm about to bear
Our baby there,
In the darkness, with the stars for light!

6. O Mar-y! O Mar-y!
Dearest, I'm so very proud of you!
You've just given birth
To the best boy on earth,
And the best boy in heaven too!

7. O Jo-seph! O Jo-seph!
Shepherds here have come to share our joy!
As the angels tell -
We must sing as well -
It's a miracle from God! Amen!

As the angels tell -
We must sing as well -
It's a miracle from God! Amen!

8. IN THE DAYS OF KING HEROD

1. In the days of king Herod,
Those Wise Men travelled far
To Jerusalem, where they
Wondered where the King might be?
The King they sought for was Jesus,
Though they knew not at the time,
And they found Him in a stable,
Fell down, and worshipped Him.

2. Herod said, "When you find him
Let me know, that I may come
Too, and worship Him!" So they
Went to Bethlehem, as planned.
The star above had guided them,
And seemed to stop and stay
Right over the place
Where the blessed Jesus lay.

3. When the Wise Men discovered Jesus,
They knelt down to give their gifts.
There was gold for the King of kings
To express His royalty.
And there was frankincense, fragrant,
A perfumed choice they gave,
And myrrh, the strangest gift of all,
More in keeping with the grave.

4. In a dream they were advised to
Go home another way.
In a dream Mary's husband Joseph
Was advised to do the same.
"Escape to Egypt!" was the message,
"For King Herod's going to kill
All baby boys under two,
And that means your baby, too!"

5. After Herod had died,
Joseph had another dream.
"It's safe now for you to travel
And go back to Nazareth!"
So they went back there in safety
To Nazareth once more,
And lived in peace, there, as a family
In their new home, Galilee.

9. WISE MEN GAVE THEIR GIFTS.

1. Wise Men gave their gifts.
And angels sang 'Alleluia!'
And the star shone above the stable,
And as fast as they were able
The shepherds returned.
They told everyone what they had learned.

2. 'In a manger, in a stable,
We saw God in human form!
We saw Joseph, and his dear wife Mary -
And that's where Jesus was born!

3. You'll just have to believe it!
So try to understand!
But we saw it with our very own eyes -
So, spread it through the land!'

4. Then the three Wise Men set off home,
But they went back by another route.
They had heard about Herod's envy.
They were warned that he was angry,
And in Bethlehem he
Slaughtered every boy under two.
　　　But he died before he knew -
　　　That Jesus lives in me and you!

10. WE COME TONIGHT

1. We come tonight
Because we believe in Jesus!
We come because
We celebrate His birth!
We come to sing
With the host of heaven
Allelu-ia, alllelu!

2. Tonight we think
Of that lowly stable.
The manger there,
That served Him as a bed.
Is there no room
In our hearts for Jesus?
We ask this, each Christmas night!

3. We feel the power
Of His Holy Spirit.
It's at this hour
That we sense His touch.
He will return
Some day - we don't know when,
But we'll be ready, when he comes.

4. We come tonight
Because we believe in Jesus!
We come because
We celebrate His birth!
We come to sing
With the host of heaven
Allelu-ia, alllelu!

THE 2006 PHARADAY LECTURE
at St. John's College, Cambridge

A full list of references to the words in italics - found in hymns, psalms, and prayerbooks - is available on request.

Maybe you have been reading the newspapers recently? In Jerusalem, we *praise him that he made The Sun.* What a wonderful paper that is! And, talking about the Mayor of Jerusalem again, I found on his person last week copies of *The Star, and The Sun.* He had been taking part in a tug of war, and the headline was, *"The Holy City shall take up the strain!"* Good, eh?

On the political scene, he was hoping that *Labour would end with sunset ray,* and that *rest should come to the weary.* However, *such a light affliction shall help him win so great a prize,* and it had also been a very good *autumn for the Liberals.* But *there, no night brings rest from Labour. "Come, Labour on!"* were the headlines of the papers that day. *"What can we do to prosper and increase the brotherhood of all mankind?"* he wonders, committing himself to *Labour night and day.*

Labour is sweet, for thou hast toiled! "O happy if ye Labour!" was his campaign motto. "After the forthcoming elections," says Grace, encouraging him, *"thou mays't smile at all thy foes!"* Thinking that he could even walk on water if he wanted to, she adds, *"Move on the water's face, bearing the lamp of Grace!"* That's nice, isn't it!

But he hadn't been feeling so well recently. The doctor says that the trouble is not so much in the mind, but in the body. He *has a weary brain, and troubled breast,* and such a combination is not good.

His wife tells him that he should take it easy, but all this does is to aggravate him. The doctor advises Grace to *praise him for his grease and fever.* He says to her, *"bid thou the blasts of discord cease!"* - and, being a bit on the selfish side, he *calls the hours his own.*

The Mayor really harks back to the time of his youth, when he was quite accomplished as a skier. *When in the slippery paths of youth* - not for him the nursery slopes - *with heedless steps he ran!* Once he had a serious accident. He goes so fast that he bumps into his brother, and *bends on earth a brother's eye* - which put him in hospital for several weeks!

He's taken to keeping-fit these days. He likes nothing better than to *wrestle and fight and pray!* But his figure is not what it used to be. In fact, his dear wife *Grace is found to be just as plenteous* as he is. He thinks that Grace weighs more when she's made herself up. When she wears *the jewels of right celestial worth* that he gave her for Christmas, her family feels quite put out, particularly her *spangled sisters bright.*

"Through every period of my life" says Grace, "you used to look at me adoringly, and in my younger days, at least *thou didst note my working breast,"* and you utterly adored my *natal star. "Arise, O morning star!"* you used to say. But all you seem to want to do these days is to *ponder nothing earthly-minded." "Take possession of my breast,"* she teases, *"and just lay down thy head upon my breast!"*

She knows he *loves the lowly spot.* "Take me, dearest," she urges - *heated in the chase* - *"just as I am, of that free love,* in which we both used to revel!" Then she worries that *the arm of flesh will fail him,* and she knows that *she dare not trust her own.*

"It is my chief complaint that my love is weak and faint," he says. *"Our beauties are but for a day!"* she sighs. "Yet, *who can tell the pleasure?"*

"All ye men of tender heart, cast care aside, lean on thy guide!" she urges, *"and knit our hearts in one!"* "At least, *give me to bear thy easy yoke!"* he replies, knowing that *it calms the troubled breast.*

"But, my dear, *why are thy bounties all in vain, before unwilling guests displayed?"* "Oh, what the heck! *multiply our Graces!"* he muses, knowing that *Grace never fails, from age to age.* *"Faint not, nor fear,"* she thinks, *"his arms are near!"*

"I see the sights that dazzle, the tempting sounds I hear! To walk with thee is heaven! Your love is so strong, dear, *how firm to the end!"* O happy servant he, in such a posture found! *"Never quench our fevered thirst of pleasure!"* she drools, *yearning strong* as ever, and *spreads her wings of peaceful love.* And with that, she *broke the fetters that enthralled her.* *"I delivered thee when bound,"* he reminds her. Rest comes at length, as they hand in hand agree.

He harks back to the past, and sighs, *"Perverse and foolish oft I strayed,* when *I loved the garish day,* and the *pleasures pure and undefiled.* And *shall not we from earthly joys abstain?"* Grace replies, however, *"What peaceful hours I once enjoyed!"* He concludes by saying, "So, dear Grace, *with thee beside me, I shall never stray* now!" *"When comes the promised time"* he wondered.

He so much wanted *Grace to persevere.* *The secret of thy love unfold, he begs her.* His eyes return to gazing on those *deep unfathomable mines* in front of him. *"Who are these, in dazzling brightness?* he asks himself.

Soon the night of weeping shall be the morn of song, he
reckons. In any case, "*he wants not friends that have thy
love,*" he says to himself. "*I will not let thee go,*" he
reassures her. "*Now to be thine, and thine alone!*"
And this is the routine *love-song which they bring.*
However, *by many deeds of shame, we learn that love
grows cold!*

So then, what does the Mayor do day by day? He has to
combat the rising crime in the city. An arsonist burned
down the sports pavilion last year, *with inextinguishable
blaze.* It was a disaster. It is also reported that shoplifting is
much on the increase, with *laden souls by thousands
stealing.*

The police came across *the benediction shed* chockablock
with contraband pork, labelled *'Treasure Bore.'* "We must
do all we can" said the Mayor, "to *confound their knavish
tricks!*" Although, "*I see the sights that dazzle, the
tempting sounds I hear!*"

He has been trying to improve the city's music recently, as
a result of certain adverse criticisms of the city choir. "*Let
our choir new anthems raise!*" said a spokesman for the
band. "*Go, work today!*"

"*Who are all this glorious band?*" he asked. "They are *the
saintly band,*" was the reply of *the captains. The saints
uplift their voice,* and request that there should now be
loud organs and sweet harps provided.

The Mayor then suggested that *the saints on earth should
in concert sing with those whose work is done,* but
unfortunately, this, too, fell on deaf ears. "*Ye that are men
now serve him!*" urges the band captain. "*The harpers I
might hear, harping on harps of gold!*" They were
beautifully dressed, too, *the matrons, virgins, and the little
maidens.*

"Take your golden lyres," he said, *"and strike each cheerful chord!"* Later on, he said to Grace, "It was a *vision whence true peace doth spring!"*

That night was bitterly cold, and he had asked the foreman at the crematorium, *"How gleam the watch-fires through the night? Keep me burning till the break of day!"* But when he got home, he still felt cold. In order to get the fire going, he *lights The Evening Star* - being the best newspaper for the job. Then he has to read the kids a story, before they go to bed. "No more *dismal stories,* Dad!" says the littlest one, who likes the scariest stories best. *No lions, giants, goblins or foul fiends can daunt his spirit!*

"Time for bed now," says the Mayor. *"Christian children all must be mild, good, and obedient!"* he tells them. He clutches them *to the father's breast,* which they think is quite *heavenly. And he leads his children on, to the place where he is gone.*

There's just time to put-on the washing machine. "This detergent is fantastic at *purging our stains!"* he tells Grace. But he can't hang the washing out at night, because of *the copious shower* that came down unexpectedly. Grace wouldn't like *men to see her sore opprest!*

Tomorrow is a big day for the Mayor. He hopes to catch *the seraph train* for an important business meeting by the coast, as he as missed *the angelic train,* and *the slothful cannot join his train.* En route, he will no doubt see *the sailors* being *guarded, as they toss on the deep blue sea.* It was *the golden evening,* as he looked across the sea. *"Brighton's* somewhere over there, he thought, *in the west!"*

"Ah Grace," he smiles, "tomorrow will be *the glorious unknown morrow!"* and then, aside, he says to himself, "I hope the food will have improved on the train. *I hope, at least, for richer food than this!"*

64

The Mayor likes to visit the pub regularly. It is good for his image. *"Open now The Crystal Fountain!"* he thunders to the landlord, because *the slow watches of the night* have delayed the opening hour. *Late in time behold him come,* rasps the Mayor, checking the clock. *"Angels, sing on, your faithful watches keeping!"* he exclaims. The landlord appears, unwashed and unshaven, and apologises profusely, *"Thou art very weary, and I was weary too! Oh, rest beside the weary road,"* he beckons. "Sorry to have kept you waiting. I have been tied up with *the trivial round and the common task!"*

Maybe, one sunny day, the Mayor visits some other pub than *The Crystal Fountain.* They played them at darts last week, and the referee *ascribed their conquest to The Lamb.* "OK," he chuckles, from now on, "s*o purer light shall mark the road that leads me to The Lamb* instead!"

"What are you having?" asks the landlord, because this is the place where *thirsting souls receive supplies, and sweet refreshment find.*

"A pint of *mild,"* he says as *he lays his glory by,* and then decides instead that this is *the bitter weather. "The bud may have a bitter taste, but sweet will be the Flowers,* please, landlord."

Knocking back pints and chasers, *sweetly distilled in the dew and the rain,* he says, *"This shall calm our trembling breath!"* Being the Mayor, he asks one of his friends to pay the bill. "Be a *love that pays the price,"* he coaxes, "and pay in gold, *casting down the golden crowns around the glassy sea!"*

Seeing him stumble a little, the landlord exhorts him - *"Stand up, stand up!"* - but it is too late. *"Let not my slippery footsteps slide, and hold me lest I fall,"* begs the Mayor, as he sinks to the ground. With sadness, he recalls only too well *the slippery paths of youth.*

65

"He that is down need fear no fall!" replies the landlord, except that the *cherubim and seraphim* are always *falling down.* "I do find it hard to get up," he admits.

"Weak is the effort of my heart!" *"Gird up your loins, as in his sight!* This way, Mayor," coaxes the landlord. "First door on the left, for *all ye who seek for sure relief!"* The Mayor noticed a distinct smell of *rushing wind that art so strong.* "You'll be all right, *when the flood is past!"* was the final comment of the landlord. But, worse still, the chain refused to work. *"Who fixed this floating ball!"* he complains.

But then, when he looked around the floor, *the sick - o lawks! - around him lay, in frail earthen vessels and things of no worth.* "Watch by the sick!" warns the landlord. When he found that he had stepped in it, he said, *"Foul, I to the fountain fly!"* And *there, from care released,* he took only a minute or two to *gird up his loins.*

"Smarten up a bit! *Come, thy suit prepare!"* says the landlord. "And wash your *soiled face* too, while you are about it!"

Leaving the warmth of the pub, *in vain the surge's angry shock* caused him to gasp a bit for breath. But the kindly landlord sees him on his way, and laughs, *"Shout, while ye journey home! There,* at least, *no cloud nor passing vapour dims the brightness of the air. Nor shall your sword sleep in your hand!"*

My friends, I trust that you have enjoyed my lecture this year about the wonderful city of Jerusalem? I look forward to addressing you all again next year! Good night!

Professor Sniwdoog Hw Rehpotsirch
(St. John's College, Cambridge, UK,
1955-1958)

BETHLEHEM IN ISLEHAM
(I composed and sang this new carol for Christmas 2007)

1. There is a special place in Bethlehem
Where it is thought that Jesus Christ was born.
It has a charm that's all its own,
Where we believe the Seed was sown   *[one beat's pause]*
So long ago – yet, seems like yesterday.

2. This place is sadly one of bitter strife
Where different faiths do not see eye to eye.
But there is still a chance, a hope
That one day we will learn to cope,   *[one beat's pause]*
And that we'll learn to live in harmony.

[key change]

3. On Christmas night, we focus on His birth,
A festival for friendship, and for fun.
A time when families unite,
A time to celebrate The Light,   *[one beat's pause]*
A time for giving unreservedly.

4. When we put Jesus first, and others next,
And last of all, that's where we put ourselves!
This is the way that Jesus taught.
We know that it's the way we ought   *[one beat's pause]*
To make the world a better, better place.

5. [one verse, of music only, follows]

67

6.There is a special place in *Isleham,
It's in our hearts that Jesus Christ is born.
It means that everything we do
Must be the best, and just for You.   *[one beat's pause]*
So peace on earth, goodwill to all mankind!

* You may substitute the name of your own parish church here.

WHILE SHEPHERDS WATCHED THEIR FLOCKS BY NIGHT

This was a satirical attack on the fashionable policy of creating Groups within the Church of England, arguing instead that the sheep thrive on knowing their own shepherds, and vice-versa!

Once upon a time, there was a shepherd of the sheep - a good and trusty man, who tended his flock well.

One day, upon taking conversation with two other shepherds, our friends agreed upon the pooling of their resources, for reasons well known to them, but scarcely understood by the lowly sheep.

Much time was subsequently devoted to travelling backwards and forwards, and to meetings and conferences. This pleased the three men greatly. But it did not please the lowly sheep, for they were barely able to maintain the numbers of the flock, while the flow of words between the three shepherds increased by three hundred per cent!

Some time later, the three happy shepherds were again at market - devising, I suppose, more and more ways of selling the lowly sheep down the line. And while the sheep themselves were becoming even more suspicious of what increasingly devious moves their masters were about to make, the three shepherds came upon other three. All six of the shepherds at once shook hands on a deal, and grouped together into one single Groupfold, with much noise heard in the right places, of course.

As the time taken up in conferences and meetings increased, so the flow of words increased proportionately. It meant that each shepherd found that he was now faced with an altogether new anxiety, of only being allowed to say a sixth of what he wanted to say in the time allotted to him by the other five shepherds.

The only other alternative meant that each shepherd became most unpopular, by making the meetings six times longer. Back at home, the lowly sheep - the sole reason why the shepherds existed - were still barely able to maintain the numbers of the flock.

Many years elapsed, and the numerous Groupfolds throughout the length and breadth of the land at last decided to become one large Fold. However, as the days passed, it was inevitable that the 15,000 shepherds would come across severe stumblingblocks. They began to discover to their surprise that it was not only 15,000 times more difficult to say what they had wanted to say, but they found that, if they were allowed to speak at all, they had to wait 15,000 times longer to say it.

It also meant that they now required 15,000 more meetings than they had ever needed before, if the Fold was to be at all democratically organised. Nor was the time taken up in travelling anything short of 15,000 times more than before, backwards and forwards from conference to commission, from sub-committee to executive committee, while the lowly sheep were still barely able to maintain the numbers of the flock.

Presently, one wise and incredibly brave shepherd suggested that, instead of all 15,000 shepherds having to meet in one huge Fold, it would surely be simpler if they divided themselves up into two Archfolds, synodically or what you will - the one at Canterbury, and the other at York.

Meanwhile, the lowly sheep, who had just about survived the lack of shepherding which had smitten the country drastically, and were still barely able to maintain the numbers of the flock, noticed that sheep-morale was sinking lower and lower.

And then, something extraordinary happened. As the idea of the two Archfolds took on, throughout the length and breadth of the land, the shepherds again began to tire of travelling so much, backwards and forwards to the various conferences at Canterbury and at York, especially in the winter months. So they hit upon the brainwave of dividing themselves into a number of far more manageable smaller units, which they called Diocesanfolds.

These Diocesanfolds were in turn later subdivided into Ruralfolds, each with a Ruralshepherd as the chief administrator and chief pastor.

Years elapsed, and the sheep were encouraged perceptibly by the greater attention given to them by the shepherds. The latter, of course, were able to afford far more time for the sheep, on account of not having to travel backwards and forwards to conferences and the like.

And hence the numbers of the flocks began to increase significantly by ones and twos, proportionate to the response shown by the lowly sheep to the greater faithfulness of their shepherds.

And you can guess the rest. The shepherds were still shepherds, after all, and the sheep were still sheep - which is what united them anyway! So the numbers of the flocks soon became great enough for the happy shepherds to divide up into even smaller units still.

They called the smaller units Parishfolds, the great advantage being that the happy shepherd could now know all his lowly sheep by name, and the Parishfold was small enough for the lowly sheep to know their happy shepherd!

In the end, talk was rarely heard again of the erstwhile idea of Groupfolds. The lowly sheep had never wanted them anyway. Furthermore, each shepherd now fully understood the idea of Groupfolds to be ludicrous if taken to its logical conclusions, as shown above. And, anyway, by now the shepherds suspected that, if the Parishfolds were almost certainly not the will of God as revealed to them by their former experiences, - then at the least they were certainly the will of the lowly sheep.

Whether it was coincidence, or what, we don't know - but the Parishfold shepherds began to recollect what it was for which they were originally Ordained - namely to tend the lowly sheep. The sheep, of course, having had this in mind for many years, showed their gratitude by increasing the numbers of the flocks, and by being ever more responsive to the encouragement of the Parishfold shepherds.

Shepherds and sheep both agreed that they were both infinitely wiser now than ever before, and happily put the whole thing behind them, as having been an awful waste of everybody's time and money.

BAAAAA-*AAAA*-*AAA*-*AA*-*A*

OH I SAY, OH I SAY!

Composed and sung by me at the 2001 annual dinner of the St. John's College Cambridge Choir Association, in the presence of Dr George Guest - to the tune of 'Oh I say! Oh I say!' - from 'Round The Horn.')

1. Our Choir is so famous, it's top of the list!
        Oh I say, oh I say!
St. John's College, Cambridge will never be missed!
        Oh I say, oh I say!
There was a suggestion in one-nine-nine-one
To contact old Choristers, just for the fun
Of making quite sure that we stay Number One!
        Oh I say, oh I say!

2. A group started up forty-five years ago
        Oh I say, oh I say!
Of old Choral scholars, and present ones too
        Oh I say, oh I say!
We staggered along for a few years, they say
It should have done well, but it faded away.
But now we've re-grouped! We're SJC CA!
        Oh I say, oh I say!

3. We're frightfully proud of our CA website
        Oh I say, oh I say!
Just visit our home page, by day or by night
        Oh I say, oh I say!
The whole of the world can find out what we do!
The old choir was good, but then so is the new!
And the place up the road has become number two!
        Oh I say, oh I say!

4. We really are privileged meeting like this
        Oh I say, oh I say!
It's so nice to show that we're backing up Chris
        Oh I say, oh I say!
The Choir's reputation is second to none
Throughout every continent, - truly, we've done
The best in the world. We've got Kings on the run!
        Oh I say, oh I say!

5. Our membership totals increase every week
        Oh I say, oh I say!
Three hundred at present, but lots more to seek
        Oh I say, oh I say!
We've started a Bursary scheme, so that we
Can help our choir members' careers, don't you see
We're all jolly grateful to dear SJC!
        Oh I say, oh I say!

6. Tonight we are honoured with George as our Guest
        Oh I say, oh I say!
Because of his vision, St. John's is the best
        Oh I say, oh I say!
We sang with him, ate with him, drank with him too,
For years he put up with us all, me and you!
We owe him so much! Thank you George! Yes it's true!
        Oh I say, oh I say!

7. So please charge your glasses, and raise them with me
        Oh I say, oh I say!
A toast to this group, CA of SJC
        Oh I say, oh I say!
We wish you success in the years now ahead
We want you to know it's all true what we've said
St. John's College, Cambridge - The Leader, not led!
        Oh I say, oh I say!

A PLEA TO THE ELY DIOCESE 2001

(composed and sung by me at the
Annual Parochial Church Meeting,
to the tune of 'Much Binding In The Marsh.')

1. At Saint Andrew's Isleham,
Our problem is – we have no central heating!
At Saint Andrew's Isleham,
It's freezing cold in church to hold a meeting!
> We wrap-up well with scarves and gloves,
> hot-water bottles, too,
> We sit next to each other
> as it's warmer in the pew;
> But what we need is money –
> fifty thousand pounds will do
At Saint Andrew's, Isleham.
> We need assistance
> At Saint Andrew's, Isleham!

2. At Saint Andrew's, Isleham,
We've only eighty people who are voters.
Oh – at Saint Andrew's, Isleham
It's way beyond our means to pay our Quotas!
> With gift-aid as our policy,
> we try to make it fit.
> We don't have many earners,
> and they do their little bit,
> But pensioners and kids
> are finding it so cold to sit
At Saint Andrew's, Isleham,
> The kids and codgers
> At Saint Andrew's, Isleham.

3. At Saint Andrew's, Isleham,
It would be rather nice to have a Vicar!
At Saint Andrew's, Isleham,
To heat our church would probably be quicker!
We're getting rather weary
as we plod on week by week.
We've tried to win the Lottery
without a single squeak.
The chances of success are non-existent,
so there's pique
At Saint Andrew's, Isleham,
We're getting anxious,
At Saint Andrew's, Isleham.

4. At Saint Andrew's, Isleham,
The parish hangs together as by magic.
At Saint Andrew's, Isleham,
The future looks to us extremely tragic.
No matter how we struggle,
things get far worse day by day;
It looks to us as if we'll never
ever pay our way,
Unless we get a miracle –
what are we going to say
At Saint Andrew's, Isleham?

Please keep us open,
At Saint Andrew's, Isleham.

Just fifty thousand,
At Saint Andrew's, Isleham.

Lord hear our prayers,
At Saint Andrew's, Isleham.

VICAR'S REPORT TO THE APCM 2001

(Composed and *actually sung* by me - instead of reading a lengthy Report in prose - to the tune of *'Oh I say! Oh I say!'* - from *'Round The Horn.')*

To my knowledge, *no Vicar has <u>ever</u> sung Annual Reports!* So these ones must be *an absolute first* in the history of the Church Of England!

1. A year has gone by since I said this before
       Oh I say! Oh I say!
Our numbers are smaller and there's room for more
       Oh I say! Oh I say!
       The children are happy in coming to church
       The boiler caught fire leaving us in the lurch
       Your Priest is in charge, and he's still on his perch
Oh I say! Oh I say!

2. The work is being shared by a pitiful few
       Oh I say! Oh I say!
It really would help if we could count on you
       Oh I say! Oh I say!
       The organist left, so we sing on our own
       The choir has diminished with never a groan
       But Jenny's piano has heightened the tone
Oh I say! Oh I say!

3. No longer do we use the dear ASB
       Oh I say! Oh I say!
We've got Common Worship, and its plain to see
       Oh I say! Oh I say!
       The structure is different, the words are the same
       The publishers like it , - for money's their game,
       The man in the street's unaware of its name
Oh I say! Oh I say!

(up a semitone)

4. It's really quite fun on our church PCC
       Oh I say! Oh I say!
We get through the business by nine fifty three
       Oh I say! Oh I say!
       Dear Wenda as Chairman,
       the team works like hell
       With Robert as back-up, the church has to gel -
       There's no Other Business these days, -
       just as well!
Oh I say! Oh I say!

5. The pastoral work trundles on week by week
       Oh I say! Oh I say!
We baptise the babies before they can speak
       Oh I say! Oh I say!
       We marry them, bury them, counsel them too,
       We catch up with everyone, - certainly true
       So don't count your chickens, for one day it's *you!*
Oh I say! Oh I say!

6. The seasons roar by at a staggering pace
       Oh I say! Oh I say!
With Christmas just over, it's Easter we face
       Oh I say! Oh I say!
       The housegroups in Lent taught us all such a lot
       We never imagined the knowledge we got
       There's no one around who dare call us a clot!
Oh I say! Oh I say!

(up a semitone)

7. The Bishop of Ely was sorry to leave
        Oh I say! Oh I say!
It's Anthony now, but we miss Bishop Steve
        Oh I say! Oh I say!
        His Isleham visit was welcomed, last Fall
        The school children showed him
         their brand new school hall
        He's seen every parish,
         he's been to them all
Oh I say! Oh I say!

8. The Christmas Christingle was second to none
        Oh I say! Oh I say!
The church was so full, it was all such great fun
        Oh I say! Oh I say!
        The children were careful with candles alight
        And no one got hurt, and no hair set alight
        For the Children's Society thinks it's all right
Oh I say! Oh I say!

9. Our Deanery contacts are showing the strain,
        Oh I say! Oh I say!
We've tried ecumenical links with Pound Lane,
        Oh I say! Oh I say!
        Top Chapel is noticeable, being so near,
        Much harder to park outside church
         when they're here,
        But we get on quite well, and we don't shed a tear!
Oh I say! Oh I say!

(up a semitone)

10. Our young married couples are few on the ground,
Oh I say! Oh I say!
But Sunday School children are always around,
Oh I say! Oh I say!
They witness in church standing up for The Lord,
We honestly say that not one of them's bored,
And the chocolate at Easter is always adored!
Oh I say! Oh I say!

11. Our ringers we have to import from elsewhere
Oh I say! Oh I say!
They practice on Mondays, but Sundays are rare
Oh I say! Oh I say!
Occasional weddings and special days few,
The bells are well-oiled, and the ringers are too
It keeps them amused,
gives them something to do!
Oh I say! Oh I say!

12. We've launched out in faith in two thousand and one
Oh I say! Oh I say!
We've done quite a bit, but there's tons to be done
Oh I say! Oh I say!
So long as you've got me, I'll give you my best
We work as a team here if you do the rest
But the good Lord above sets the one final test!
Oh I say! Oh I say!

TRAD AND NOVO

**This satirical skit was written at a time when
all that I stood for as a Vicar
was being challenged by the diehards -
particularly three people
whose dinosauric influence upon the congregation
was such that no one dared to stand up to them.**

DRAMATIS PERSONAE:

TRAD: a PLO traditionalist *(A member of
The Prayerbook Liberation Organisation!)*
NOVO: a modernist

"In the beginning was the Word . . ."

Trad: We love the lovely language . . .

Novo: What? Like *"The Word?"* what does *that* mean?

Trad: "The Word" means *Jesus.*

Novo: Then why not say *Jesus?*

Trad: Because we love the lovely language . . .

Novo: It surely makes more sense to say,

"*Jesus* was in the beginning . . ."

Trad: Oh no, we still prefer the lovely language.

*"And the word was with God,
and the word was God . . ."*

Trad: It's so refreshing to hear the lovely language used

Novo: You mean that Jesus *was* God?

Trad: No, we mean that Jesus *is* God

81

Novo: Well why say he *"WAS"* when you mean he *IS* God?

Trad: The language is so beautiful, that's why! . . .

Novo: So, "Jesus was in the beginning,

and Jesus was with God, and Jesus is God." *Yes?*

Trad: Yes, but the old language sounds

so much more beautiful . . .

Novo: Even if you don't understand it?

Trad: We *DO* actually understand it.

Novo: But you had to *explain* what it really meant!

Trad: Well, never mind that. The language is so beautiful.

It flows. It's so refreshing! It's so good to find a church that

still uses the lovely old language. So measured.

So full of meaning. We prefer the *old* words, you see.

Novo: You prefer the *old* words:

So Jesus is an *old man,* then?

Trad: No, silly! When we say *"Word,"*

we don't mean *word,* but *Jesus.*

Novo: Then why don't you say so?

Trad: Because we love the lovely old language . . .

Novo: You mean the lovely *wordy language?*

Trad: Yes. No. Yes, of course, but we still prefer

the lovely *old* words . . .

Novo: Why do you use *modern* words to speak to me then, if you prefer the *old* words?

Trad: Because we only use the old words *in church.*

Novo: So if you prefer the old words, why do you use 1662 English? Why not Latin? Or Greek? Or, better still, Aramaic? Surely 1662 English is rather *modern,* when you consider that the Church managed in other languages for *1600 years* before then?

Trad: Well, the lovely language of Cranmer's beautiful prose was good enough for our fathers and grandfathers, and that's why it's good enough for us!

Novo: But you don't use it when you speak to *me*, do you?

Trad: Of course not! You're not *GOD,* you see!

Novo: So God only understands *the lovely old language,* then? God only understands *Shakespearean English?* How ever did He understand 1600 years' worth of *Latin* before *that,* then?

Trad: He didn't *need* to understand it.

Novo: Then why does *He* need to be spoken to, in Shakespearean English, in 2008?

Trad: Because the language is so lovely, so measured, so beautiful. And God deserves all things beautiful . . .

Novo: All things bright and beautiful?

Trad: Yes. No. Yes! Of *course* He does!

(**Trad** *breaks into song,*
to the tune of *All things bright and beautiful . . .*):

> Words must be traditional,
> We must use Cranmer's prose.
> Measured, lovely, beautiful,
> The language really flows!

> Our fathers loved the *old* words,
> Our granddads loved them too;
> The old words served them well, so
> they're good enough for you
> > and me,
> > so –

> Words must be traditional,
> We must use Cranmer's prose.
> Measured, lovely, beautiful,
> It's all our *old God* knows!

Novo: *You win!*

VICAR'S REPORT TO THE APCM 2002

*(Composed and actually sung by me -
instead of reading a lengthy Report -
to the tune of 'Land of hope and glory')*

1. At our Annual Meeting, in two thousand and two,
We are still without heating! What a how-d-you-do!
But I'd like to thank you for your loyalty here.
We can't do without you! Just keep worshipping here!
        Keep the name of Jesus
        foremost in your lives!

2. Our young people love to take their part each week.
Church is so much fun, now – you should hear them speak!
Last year had its sadness. Several people died.
But we shared the gladness of those married, beside
        Six young people Confirmed,
        and new folk joining us, too!

3. Lent, this year was a Fun Quiz. Several people took part.
Halftime drinks brought a warm fizz,
laugh and learn is the art!
Thirty Penny Club members raised two thousand pounds,
Four five pennies for cuppas, ten pence for a main meal:
        It's so very easy –
        money simply pours in!

4. Pound Lane, and the Baptists
joined the Day of World Prayer,
Also, on Good Friday – time that Christians should share!
HC every Sunday, ten o-clock on the dot,
BCP and CW – we use both, a lot!
        Family Service monthly –
        that's the pattern we've got!

5. Highlights were the Carols, Taizé Festival of Light,
Toy Epiphany Service, Mothering Sunday right.
Easter Day Communion with the Isleham Creed
And the Isleham Carol, mini-HC indeed,
> And the Easter crosses –
> chocolate eggs all inside!

6. Our Electoral Roll now is a working list
Though our numbers halved, it represents activists!
Junior church is increasing, bells are ringing Sundays,
Sidesmen work to a rôta, so do those who pray,
> Servers, readers, refreshments –
> we enjoy work and play!

7. Soon we'll be a part of The Three Rivers Group,
Chippenham, Fordham, and Kennett,
Snailwell join in a loop.
What will be the outcome? No one seems to know,
But we hope our Church will keep on wanting to grow!
> As your Priest-in-Charge,
> I'll serve you till I go!

8. We are both so happy working with you here,
Coming out of retirement, keeps me younger, I hear!
While we work as a team, we pull together as one,
And, although we're few, we get the business done!
> So, thank God for our Church here!
> Annual Meetings are fun!

VICAR'S REPORT TO THE APCM 2003

*(composed and actually sung by me -
instead of reading a lengthy Report -
to the tune of 'Greensleeves.')*

1. Another year has passed us by,
We've done our best. We've had a try
To heat this church, and repair it too
And at last, we have signs of a break-through.
   But, now, put care aside,
   And thank the Lord for his blessings here.
   Thank you, for your loyalty -
   We work as a team at St. Andrew's.

2. We've lost some dear ones, but gained some new.
Our Junior Church is full of life.
We're part of 'The Three Rivers Group,'
But it hasn't made very much impact!
   June saw the three Churches meet, when
   We celebrated her fifty years -
   Queen Elizabeth's Jubilee -
   With a right royal time together.

3. The Parish Gift Day surprised us all,
And people gave very generously.
The Flower Festival filled the church
And brought life to the whole of the Parish!
   Then a Jewish film crew came,
   And filmed the Hanukkah candlestick,
   Made by some evacuees
   When they lodged at The Griffin in wartime.

4. Our Carol Service was new this time
With Soham Band accompaniment.
The Christmas trees, and the Toy Service
Were the 'high' of the Festival Season.
     In April we saw the launch
     Of the "Limerick Old Testament,"
     Written when Vicar was down to earth -
     Instead of flying his Cessna!

5. The Pancake Party and Beetle Drive
Began the Season of Lent this year.
The Vicar started to clean the streets -
Shed fourteen pounds in the process!
     The Lent Quiz was enormous fun
     As a teaching aid, and it showed us that
     Everyone has a lot to learn -
     And to do it at home was much nicer!

6. So this is going to be Our Year,
To repair the roof and the plasterwork,
And heat the church, and fill the pews,
And work hard to be Jesus' disciples!
     Although we are few in numbers
     Our strength is spirituality!
     God bless us in all we do!
     And that's my report to this Meeting!

VICAR'S REPORT TO THE APCM 2004

(composed and actually sung by me -
instead of reading a lengthy Report -
to the tune of 'Sing a song of sixpence')

1. The church is full of scaffolding, the organ's covered up;
The font is bathed in plastic
 and the place is thick with dust;
But life goes on at Isleham. We take it in our stride.
We're making sure the work gets done,
With God being on our side.
>   We're making sure the work gets done,
>   With God being on our side.

2. It doesn't seem a year ago since we launched the appeal,.
But funds came in by dribs and drabs,
 and boosted our morale.
We haven't got the hearing yet, but manage with the help
Of heaters meant for barbecues, and they work just as well!
>   Of heaters meant for barbecues,
>   And they work just as well!

3. Our junior church is lots of fun, and what we love to see
Our children taking part in Church –
the place where they should be.
We packed it out at Christmastide,
Christingle draws a crowd.
We showed some toys and brought some gifts:
 Epiphany rang loud!
>   We showed some toys and brought some gifts:
>   Epiphany rang loud!

4. We gave out 'fish' at Eastertide,
with chocolate eggs inside,
And had some fun at pancake-time,
with beetle-drives desired.
A lorry crashed into the gate and Social Centre wall;
It took a while to get it straight. It must affect us all!
    It took a while to get it straight.
    It must affect us all!

5. Last Lent, we had a parish quiz, with many taking part,
We realised there's a lot to learn, and learning is an art;
The children from our local school
came many times to church,
They tried their best to catch me out,
and knock me off my perch!
    They tried their best to catch him out,
    And knock him off his perch!

6. Gift Day last year raised lots of cash;
 the Trivia-evenings, too;
And though we need to pay our way, it's not all that we do!
We launched a group on Wednesdays,
with evenings spent in thought;
At lunchtime once again, for prayer,
we give God what we ought!
    At lunchtime once again, for prayer,
    We give God what we ought!

7. Three Clubs are in the pipeline, man,
for friends from USA;
And those who use computers
can record names day by day;
For families with Baptisms a monthly meeting too;
And start the pram Service again is what we'd like to do.
    And start the pram Service again
    Is what we'd like to do.

8. Last Lent, I went and cleaned the streets,
   filled forty plastic sacks;
And met folk on their own home ground,
with not a few wise-cracks!
The parish Registers are now in the computer stored,
It took some months of typing, but at least I wasn't bored!
>   It took some months of typing,
>   But at least he wasn't bored!

9. A lorry driver, who was Dutch, crashed into our new car;
   And tried to drive us off the road, but we survived, yes Sir!
The daily round of common tasks
   provides me with a living,
But what I like the best of all is worship, work, and giving!
>   But what we like the best of all
>   Is worship, work, and giving!

10. As future weeks go flying by,
    our church will look just so;
But what we need to do this year
   is make our numbers grow.
If each Church member brings one more
   the church will soon be full,
So God bless you in what you do,
and God bless me as well!
>   So God bless us in what we do,
>   And God bless him as well!

MY MAUNDY THURSDAY EXPERIENCE

The final Eucharist of my two years at Lincoln Theological College was an extraordinarily emotional occasion. Afterwards, at about 10pm, we all went over to Lincoln Minster for an hour's silent meditation - in complete darkness, except for one 60W light bulb at the far end of the nave.

For the first few minutes, I sat behind the choir stalls. A quarter of an hour later, I was in the process of making my way to the altar rails, but failed to notice that one of my colleagues was deep in prayer, prostrate on the chancel floor ahead of me, with his arms outstretched, his body making the shape of a cross. As the heel of my shoe ground down on the fingers of his right hand, the whole Minster was filled with a dreadful scream - a scream that could only come from a man in agony. He thanked me, later on, saying that he was glad to have had an experience of something of the pain Jesus must have felt, when the nails were hammered-in at the crucifixion.

However, after apologising profusely, I knelt at the altar rail for the remainder of the hour, meditating deeply on *The Light of Christ,* and *Jesus the Light of the world.* The more I thought about it, the more I suddenly became aware of the presence of a bright Light in front of me, about 6 feet tall and about 18 inches wide. It was so real that I could have touched *Him.* I was convinced that He was Jesus, and that *The Light of the world - The Light of Christ -* was *actually there,* with me. When the hour was up, we all returned back to College, in complete silence.

The next morning at breakfast, someone commented, "Whatever was the matter with you last night? You were blubbering like a baby!"

"I certainly was *not!*" I retorted.

"But you *were,* Christopher, you really *were!*"

He said that I was crying *in tongues* - which is certainly not my style, and I have never experienced anything like it, before or since. But those who heard me were totally convinced that what he had said was true.

I feel absolutely certain that This was the presence of Jesus Himself and, as a result, Maundy Thursday evening has always been very precious to me indeed. Although it is fifty years ago since this happened, Doreen was able to visualise what I described, and by using bleach over a background of Indian ink, managed to create an accurate picture of the *Maundy Thursday experience* that occurred that special night - something that completely changed my life!

Christopher WH Goodwins, MA(Cantab)
1964.

A FORM OF HOLY COMMUNION

Our weekly housegroup met for a year to research the origins of the Eucharist, and found it to be a most illuminating experience. As a result, we decided to see whether we could come up with a form of words that could be suitable for this part of the 21st Century - and this is the result. We used it at Rosemarkie, Scotland, when we celebrated Doreen's 70th birthday.

A TIME FOR MEDITATION

We sit in quiet reflection,
thinking about the amazingness of creation,
and we spend a moment thanking God
for being allowed to be a part of it.

[Meditational slides will be shown,
to a background of quiet reflective music.]

[Cantor starts the following hymn,
and at the second verse, one by one,
we join-in the next line, until we're all singing together.]

Be still, for the presence of the Lord, the Holy One is here.
Come bow before Him now, with reverence and fear.
In Him no sin is found. We stand on holy ground.
Be still, for the presence of the Lord, the Holy One is here.

Be still, for the glory of the Lord is shining all around.
He burns with holy fire, with splendour He is crowned.
How awesome is the sight, our radiant King of Light.
Be still, for the glory of the Lord is shining all around.

Be still, for the power of the Lord
is moving in this place.
He comes to cleanse and heal, to minister His grace.
No work too hard for Him. In faith receive from Him.
Be still, for the power of the Lord
is moving in this place.

CONFESSION
We all say together:

Dear God, acknowledging that those who don't think
that they do wrong
don't necessarily do everything right, either;
we freely confess to having erred from Your true path,
by negligently following selfish or narrow interest,
instead of opening our hearts and minds
to the greater creation with which you have blessed us.

Please help us to be tolerant
of the apparently intolerable;
to be patient with the positively exasperating;
to be charitable to the undeserving;
to be mindful of (and for) the mindless;
to be forgiving of the unforgivable;
and, above all, to increase our awareness
that we hold Your creation in stewardship for all your
creatures, now and in the future.
Please help us to be worthy of that awesome
responsibility.

There are sins we can think of,
and others we don't know about:
please include them, forgiving our ignorance.
Thank you, Lord, for your kindness.

ABSOLUTION

May God, the creator of all we are,
look favourably upon the sincerity of our confession;
forgive our transgressions;
instruct our ignorance;
and continue to show us His way to life eternal.
Through Jesus Christ, our Lord and Redeemer.
Amen.

A SHORT INTERLUDE OF MUSIC

A SPECIAL PRAYER FOR TODAY

SOME NEW TESTAMENT READINGS

Philippians 4:8 *(from the Revised Version)*

Finally, brethren,
whatsoever things are true,
whatsoever things are honourable,
whatsoever things are just,
whatsoever things are pure,
whatsoever things are lovely,
whatsoever things are of good report;
if there be any virtue,
and if there be any praise,
think on these things.

Galatians 5: 22-23 *(from the New Living Translation)*

But the Holy Spirit produces this kind of fruit in our lives:
love, joy, peace, patience, kindness, goodness,
faithfulness, gentleness, and self-control.
There is no law against these things!

John 20: 16 *(from The Bible in Limerick Verse)*

She went to the tomb Sunday morning.
The stone was removed, without warning.
She stood back in tears,
'It is I!' Mary hears -
'Your Lord is arisen! No mourning!'

John 20: 19 - 21 *(from The Bible in Limerick Verse)*

The Upper Room, Monday that week,
The doors still locked fast. Not a squeak
The Lord crossed the floor.
'I'll be with you some more!
Peace be with you!' he said. *Fantastique!*

A CELEBRATION OF THE LIFE OF JESUS

We celebrate the birth of Jesus.
[large candle is lit in prominent central position.]

Remembering what Jesus did and said in his lifetime on earth,
we now recall his death. *[Before the central candle is extinguished,*
representing the death of Jesus, one nightlight receives its flame.]

We reflect upon his resurrection. *[central candle is re-lit]*

We symbolise the sending of the Holy Spirit of the living Lord Jesus.
[each lights a nightlight from the central candle.]

We look to the time when Jesus will come again.
[All nightlights are placed in a circle around the central candle.]

WE PROCLAIM WHAT CHRISTIANS BELIEVE

We sing 'A Christian Creed.' *[Cantor leads.]*

Repeated 3 times

We be-lieve in one God, Ma-ker of heav-en and earth. Yes!

C: *We believe in one God,*
All: **We believe in one God,**

C: *We believe in Jesus,*
All: **We believe in Jesus,**

C: *And His Holy Spirit,*
All: **And His Holy Spirit,**
Maker of heaven and earth.
Yes!

2.   **He came down from heaven,**
Mary was his mother,
By the Spirit's power,
He comes to save the world.
Yes!

up a semitone

3. But we went and killed Him,
He was dead and buried
In the tomb for three days.
Jesus is risen! Alive!
Yes!

4, Comes to His disciples,
Eats and drinks among us,
Showed his wounds to Thomas,
He is alive! That's right!
Yes!

5. We who follow Jesus,
Feel His Holy Spirit,
All the Father promised,
Happens to us today!
Yes!

6. Give your life for Jesus,
Start today to trust Him,
Pray that He will lead you,
Transform your life today!
Yes!

up a semitone

7.   **Sunday is for worship,**
Join with local Christians,
Serve our human beings,
Workers for Jesus: Unite!
Yes!

8. Turn away from evil,
Love, be kind and helpful,
Jesus is your neighbour,
This is the Christian way!
Yes!

9. Find Him in the Bible,
Find Him in the workplace,
Find Him in your household:
Jesus will shine in your eyes!
Yes!

up a semitone

10. Soon His Second coming,
Any day we'll meet Him,
We'll be there to greet Him!
Jesus, the Light of the world!
Yes!
YES!

WE SPEND A TIME OF PRAYER
IN GOD'S PRESENCE

We attach our personal prayers to the Cross,
after which Intercessions are made.

WE SHARE A MEAL

The following is a symbolic version of the Jewish Passover
Seder, or ritual meal, similar to that which was eaten at The
Last Supper, consisting of:
LAMB: the word passover applies to the Lamb of sacrifice
as well as to the deliverance from Egypt and to the feast
itself.
UNLEAVENED BREAD: called bread of affliction
because it recalls the unleavened bread prepared for the
hasty flight by night from Egypt.
BITTER HERBS: we use radishes, as a reminder of the
bitterness of slavery and suffering in Egypt.
GREEN HERBS: to be dipped in salt water. Salt water
represents tears of sorrow shed during the captivity of the
Lord's people.
HAROSETH: a mixture of chopped apples, nuts, cinnamon
and wine, represents the mortar used by Jews in building
palaces and pyramids of Egypt during their slavery.
WINE: we drink one sip (of grape juice) at the
Consecration, and three more as 'Toasts' at the end of the
meal.

THE EUCHARISTIC PRAYER.

We meet here to celebrate the life of Jesus.
We meet here to thank God for being chosen to be a part of
His creation.
We meet here to receive the power of the Holy Spirit of the
living Lord Jesus.
And we meet here to share our Christian beliefs
with anybody we meet, wherever we happen to be.
We share the excitement of Mary Magdalene,
who was first to see the risen Lord Jesus.
We know how the Resurrection absolutely convinced John,
and Peter,
and Paul, and the other close friends of Jesus.

We know how the resurrection of Jesus convinced 500
people at once, at Pentecost.
We know how Thomas, *without a shadow of doubt,* was
able to say to the risen Jesus, "My *Lord, and* my *God!"*

We thank God for the way in which countless people have
lived and worked and died for Jesus. We re-dedicate
ourselves here today – because Jesus has no eyes but our
eyes, no hands but our hands, no feet but our feet, to do His
work on earth.

We therefore state that *we too* believe that *Jesus is God,*
and we are glad to tell the whole world that we share his
life today, as Christians have done for the past twenty
centuries.

Listen to what St. Paul said:
1 Corinthians 11:20-26 *(New Living Translation)*

For I pass on to you what I received from the Lord himself.
On the night when he was betrayed,
the Lord Jesus took some bread
and gave thanks to God for it.

Then he broke it in pieces and said,
"This is my body, which is given for you.

Do this *[break the bread here]* to remember me."

*[The various seder foods are arranged on the bread,
a piece of which is passed to each person.]*

[When ready, we all say,]
"The body of Christ keep us in eternal life."

*[A short pause, with reflective music while the food is
eaten,
after which the prayer continues:]*

In the same way, he took the cup of wine after supper,
saying,
"This cup is the new covenant between God and his
people—
an agreement confirmed with my blood.
Do this *[consecrate the wine here]* to remember me
as often as you drink it."
For every time you eat this bread and drink this cup,
you are announcing the Lord's death [and resurrection]
until he comes again.

*[A small glass of grape juice is poured out for each
person.]*

[When ready, we all say,]
"The blood of Christ keep us in eternal life."

*[A short pause, and then follow **three toasts, from the
same glasses:**]*

The first, to Jesus: "***Jesus first!***"
The second, to the Christian Church: "***Others next!***"
The third, to our group, here: "***Ourselves last!***"

[The prayer continues:]

Without food and drink we die.
Without spiritual food and drink we die spiritually.
Spiritually, at this special meal, the bread and wine
symbolise the life of Jesus,
which we are glad to share together today.

This bread is made from the crushing of many grains of
wheat, and this wine is made from the crushing of many
grapes. As followers of Jesus, we try to crush our *old* way
of life, in order to put on His *new* way of life.

So, Lord Jesus, we feel the presence of your Holy Spirit
with us, right now.
Speak to each of us here some special words of
encouragement and hope;
And give us the strength to go out into all the world -
to transform lives,
to proclaim the good news of peace,
and to help bring about your new Kingdom on earth.

[We all say:]

Come, Lord Jesus.
Thank you, Lord Jesus.
Be with us, Lord Jesus.
Amen.

THE BLESSING

The Lord bless us and keep us.
The Lord make His face to shine upon us
 and be gracious unto us.
The Lord lift up the light of His countenance upon us,
and give us His peace. Now and always.
Amen.

THE GRACE

[We sing it together.]

May the grace of our Lord Jesus Christ,
and the love of God, our Father,
and the fellowship, the fellowship
 of the Holy Spirit be with us,
for evermore,
and evermore,
and evermore.
Amen.

GRUMPY OLD MAN'S SECOND ARTICLE

How many times have we been in supermarkets when a call goes out over the loudspeaker system - *"Would Mr Jones please go to the back gate, where there is a caller waiting for you"* - or something like that. And *the music* of the person's voice giving out the message is invariably the same, where the voice drops about *a musical minor fifth* after the word *'caller.'* It's what I call *the Tesco Cadence,* and you hear it in lots of shops. And I *hate* it!

The Tesco Cadence has penetrated Church life too, where the Officiant seems to read the liturgy in exactly the same way, with the dropping of the voice about a musical minor fifth towards the end of every sentence.

It really does annoy me, and I long for someone to read well. And if the voice has *got* to drop towards the end of a sentence, then please let it be *a major interval,* not a minor one - as it sounds so much less melancholic and miserable, and far more confident and pleasant to listen to.

I begin to wonder whether *the Tesco Cadence* is something that is being *taught* in Theological Colleges, rather like the parsonical voice used to be the norm in the last century - because it really is something bad, that absolutely pervades worship, whether in church or on the radio or television. At the moment, in my experience, it seems that women are the worst offenders, but *only just* in the majority!

It's the same sort of irritation I feel when I hear the church bells ring. Our local church has a peal of six bells, but the fifth one down the scale needs to be lowered by a semitone to make the peal a major one, whereas at the moment, it gives out a minor sound, and tenders the impression that the church is apologising for its message, rather than a major peal, that sounds much more confident and far more attractive. So it's not just speaking in church, but bell-ringing too that needs attention.

By contrast, I recall the most superb reading that I have ever heard, when we visited Capetown Cathedral for a morning Eucharist. The Readings were read by a most unlikely looking chap, aged about 35, with a huge mop of black tousled hair. But he read it so excellently, that we thought he must have known something about voice production, or indeed, about acting.

In fact, over coffee afterwards with the Dean, we were introduced to the reader, and learned that he was just as we had guessed - in fact, a professional actor. And the way he read the reading that morning was a shining example of how other people should read. He read with intelligence, with music, and with light and shade, and his diction was absolutely impeccable!

I recall the time when I was auditioning to be an Epilogian on Westward Television, and had to take lessons on how to sound interesting in broadcasts. Far from annoying me that I had to take lessons, I relished the idea that the way I spoke could be much improved by the expertise of those in the broadcasting Media.

And all this, despite the fact that the only prizes that I ever won at Norwich School were both for *elocution!* You see - it pays to be humble enough to learn! And having broadcast as a Television Epilogian for over seventeen years, I feel that I have *the right* to make these comments!

All these things are so important, if we want to do worship well! And *I* do, even if no one else does! Voice production should be standard training for those in public office - especially for those who lead worship in church! And in our last church, we used to hold reading practices for all those who were on the reading rôta, and it really did help! No one was too proud to learn from constructive criticism!

The same applies to those leading the intercessions. So often, their voices are so quiet that they can't be heard, or so miserable that it's hard to keep concentration. And *the Tesco Cadence* pervades the intercessions, too, as it does seem to do in so many churches and places of worship; in which case, it's high time we did something about it!

It's the same with people who read readings (never *'lessons,')* because they usually ignore the microphone, and it just makes it so very much harder to hear what they're saying. I once put a notice on the lectern and pulpit, for the benefit of visiting clergy and readers, that said, *'You've got a lovely microphone in front of you - so please USE it! Don't turn your head away from the mike, because no one will hear you!'* It worked, sometimes!

I find it so hard to hear what people are saying if they don't use the mike. In one church we go to quite often, there's an old biddy who refuses to use the mike, because she thinks that everybody can hear her in any case. But what she fails to remember is that people with hearing aids, who depend upon the looped sound system, are thereby disenfranchised by her stubbornness to use the system.

Ely Cathedral has an excellent sound system, and so does Worlington Church - our next door parish. If only all places of worship took their sound systems far more seriously!

And so, if your church is one that has a dreadful sound system, then please do something about it! And if your clergy, your officiants, your readers are guilty of *the Tesco Cadence,* then please tell them to do something about it! And if your bells ring a minor peal, then get them changed!

I may be a grumpy old man, but, in my opinion, not without good reason!

June 2014

ABOUT THE AUTHOR

Christopher William Hedley Goodwins was born in 1936 at St. Peter's Vicarage, Sparty Lea - which is a remote Allendale hamlet in the wilds of wild Northumberland. When he was just three, the family moved to Norfolk, firstly to Roydon, and then to Potter Heigham.

He spent the next ten years as a Boarder at Norwich School, distinguishing himself in very little except being Head of the School Choir, and gaining the absolute minimum of GCE O and A levels to satisfy the matriculation requirements of Cambridge University.

He was then awarded an Open Choral Scholarship to the world-famous Choir of St. John's College, as a Counter-Tenor. Graduating in 1958, he achieved a Special BA Degree in Geography and Old French Literature, coming top of his Tripos, and gaining his MA in 1961.

After Cambridge, he began his National Service as a Private in the Somerset Light Infantry at Taunton, before being Commissioned as Second Lieutenant RAEC, training as a Teacher at Beaconsfield, and finally being appointed as Education Officer attached to the Household Cavalry at Windsor.

During his last year there, he married Doreen, and the two of them took a full part in Church life at St. Michael's, Little Ilford, E12, where he was churchwarden. After a year as Education Officer to the Kuwait Government, and another year doing supply teaching at East Ham Girls' Grammar School - where he was *a Form Mistress* - he accepted a place at The Bishop's Hostel, Lincoln Theological College.

In 1964, he was Deaconed in Cromer Parish church, and Priested in 1965 in Norwich Cathedral, serving a five-year Curacy at St. Margaret's, Lowestoft and Oulton Village. During that time, he and Doreen adopted Rupert and Lulu, and in 1969 moved to Tamerton Foliot in northwest Plymouth, where he spent the next 29 years as Vicar.

On his retirement in 1998, he became Priest-in-Charge of St. Andrew, Isleham, and also qualified as a Pilot, based at Cambridge, and often flying with Doreen as his Navigatrix - until 2004, when he retired for the second time. He and Doreen have travelled extensively, broadcast often on Radio and Television, and between them have published several books.

This latest one, **THE RAMBLINGS OF A COUNTRY CLERGYMAN,** is therefore dedicated to the former Staff and Students of Lincoln Theological College, many of whom will be meeting in Lincoln in July 2014, to celebrate the fiftieth anniversary of their Ordination.

Finally, this book would not have been possible without the full support and cheerfully constructive criticism from his dear wife Doreen, the pleasure of whose company and expertise he has valued immensely for over 54 years!

So, hopefully having enjoyed reading **The Ramblings,** for a few brief moments, you will have shared something of the seventy-eight years of eccentricities that have occupied the mind of this remarkable country clergyman.

July 2014

Printed in Great Britain
by Amazon

33505616R00066